Tell Me About the Church

By Hillery C. Rice, D.D.

with a foreword by
Dr. Warren C. Roark

THE WARNER PRESS
Publication Board of the Church of God
Anderson, Indiana

Fifth Printing—30,000

PUBLISHED IN THE UNITED STATES OF AMERICA

DEDICATED

to the companion of all my joys and sorrows,
my partner in work and study, my wife,
Pauline Louise,
and to our wonderful daughter,
Carolyn Kay

CONTENTS

v

FOREWORD

This book is about the church, the greatest and most important institution in the world. The foundation for the church as a society among men was laid by the Son of God himself, and it was inaugurated under the guidance of the Holy Spirit. It was established that men might possess a spiritual habitation, a home of the soul.

The church is a redemptive force, the only redeeming agency through which the Holy Spirit works for the salvation of men. In spite of the weaknesses and shortcomings of those who, led by the Spirit of God, guide the church, it has been the blessing and inspiration of every generation. It is world-wide in its scope. It has many critics but no rivals! It is the marvel of the ages.

The church represents life-giving realities. In the midst of the variable, the transient, and the unstable, men turn to it for certainty, security, and a sense of the abiding and eternal. It has been the depository of civilization's greatest heritage and the guardian of humanity's highest ideals and aspirations.

Every true disciple of Jesus Christ should seek to learn and understand as much as possible about the church. The study will be most rewarding.

Dr. Hillery C. Rice, the author, in an interesting and convincing manner, answers many questions which people ask concerning the church. Dr. Rice is pastor of the large Park

Place Church of God in Anderson, Indiana, and for many years has been a leader in the national affairs of the Church of God movement. He is fully qualified to write on this subject.

As Luke addressed the Gospel which bears his name and the historical Book of Acts to one Theophilus, so Dr. Rice has addressed the chapters of this book to Morton, an old friend, though a new convert, who is an inquirer after truth concerning the church. The answers Mr. Rice gives to his friend's questions are clear, concise, and sound.

All who read this book will do so with profit. The information contained herein will reveal truth and light to the reader that will add much to his spiritual understanding and growth.

I am happy to commend this volume to all truth lovers everywhere.

WARREN C. ROARK, M.A., D.D.

1

WHAT IS THE CHURCH OF GOD AND WHEN DID IT BEGIN?

SUNDAY NOON

DEAR MORTON:

Your letter came yesterday and to put it mildly, it was most thrilling. First, it disclosed the good news that you have become a Christian. I have known for years that this was your deepest desire. Second, in every word you wrote and between every line there is evidence of your sincere search for Bible truth.

Do you realize, Morton, that it has been nineteen years since we were closely associated? During this time it has been good to see you occasionally, and our correspondence has been a perpetual joy to me. Well do I recall the "snap" in your eyes on that day in April, 1937, when I told you how the Lord had gloriously saved me! Six months later, when I revealed to you that God had called me to preach the gospel, you could hardly believe it—and yet you did believe it, for later many of the kind remarks you made about my becoming a minister came back to me.

Often, I have wondered if city-wide revivals have lasting value, but now that you have been converted in such a meeting, I do not wonder any longer.

So you have many, many questions to ask about the Church of God? Well, Morton, I shall be happy to try to answer

9

them, and as you suggest, we will continue our correspondence until you are better acquainted with the church. Today, I shall seek to answer your first question, which actually is a two-pronged one: "What is the Church of God and when did it begin?"

To answer this very pertinent question, it will be necessary to begin with the inception of the church, as recorded in the Bible, and give you some of its history, for only God's Word is authority on the church question. The church was conceived in the heart of God, and Jesus made it a visible reality. He said, "I will build my church; and the gates of hell shall not prevail against it" (Matt. 16:18).

In calling what he was building "the church," our Lord was using a term admirably suited to his purposes. Both the Greeks and the Jews had terms for "the called-out ones" or "the assembled." Jesus and his followers took the Greek term *ecclesia* and used it to designate this new, separated society of which Christ is the Head. It is composed of people called out of sin and confusion to be united with Christ and other Christians in a unique fellowship of the redeemed.

This new Christian body, the church, began its mission on the Day of Pentecost (see Acts 2). Though it was a brand-new movement, few having heard of it, nevertheless on that notable dedication day, "there were added unto them about three thousand souls" (vs. 41). That was the inaugural day of the church of God. Before Pentecost, Christ had commissioned his disciples to preach his gospel to all the world. On the Day of Pentecost the disciples seemed to have fully interpreted this commission for the church; from that day they earnestly brought pressure on their world for good. If you will read the Book of Acts, Morton, you will see the mighty and wonderful works of that early church. No doubt about it, those first-century followers had their signals straight; they were determined to obey their orders. For the most part human caprice would not control that church; the Spirit of God found free sway through those newborn souls.

Throughout the Book of Acts, we see the church taking form, preaching the gospel, filling its God-designed mission. It is obvious that this church was composed of all believers in the Lord everywhere; it was the church in which all members had the same experience—they were born again of the Spirit of God. They all experienced "repentance toward God, and faith toward our Lord Jesus Christ"; they practiced holy living and conversation. Christ had knowledge of the many empires, nations, and civilizations that had deteriorated and died in obscurity because of human contrivings. But He made the church of God eternal. "I will build my church, and the powers of death shall not prevail against it" (RSV[1]). His church is divine!

The conversion of Saul of Tarsus (recorded in Acts 9) gave to the world the topmost exponent of the church. Paul did not found the church, nor did he create the church idea. When he was converted the church was already here. In his own testimony, he said, "I persecuted the church of God, and wasted it" (Gal. 1:13). Nevertheless, Paul seemed to know more about the church than any other writer of his day. His revelation from God and his deep insight regarding the church were unique, to say the least. Of God's action in Christ, Paul wrote, "He has put all things under his feet and has made him the head over all things for the church, which is his body" (Eph. 1:22-23, RSV). Then from his profound insight Paul speaks of "the whole family

---

[1]This and other quotations from the Revised Standard Version in this book are copyrighted by the Division of Christian Education, NCCCUSA, and are used by permission.

in heaven and earth" (3:15). Now, this "whole family in heaven and earth" is God's family, the church of God. Christ said, "I will build my church." Paul called it "the body of Christ . . . the whole family"; therefore, it cannot be any one religious leader's body or family. It is God's family, his church, "the church of God, which he hath purchased with his own blood" (Acts 20:28).

We must keep in mind that the relationship between Christ and his church must not be strained. Christ is not only the Head of his church, but he is definitely identified with it. Harmony must exist between Christ and the church, else it cannot be the church at all. Paul, in depicting the holy relationship between Christ and his church, employed the stoutest figure at his command—the figure of husband and wife. He wrote the Ephesian Christians, "Husbands, love your wives, even as Christ also loved the church, and gave himself for it" (5:25). Both Genesis (2:24) and Matthew (19:5) say that a man shall leave father and mother and cleave to his wife and the two shall be one flesh. Paul, by using this figure shows that Christ and his church are joined together as one.

The writer of Revelation takes the husband and wife figure and lifts it to a sublime setting. "And I John saw the holy city, new Jerusalem, coming down from God out of heaven, prepared as a bride adorned for her husband" (21:2). "The holy city, the new Jerusalem" simply means the church, for it is identified with the bride of Christ. "The symbols . . . describing the new Jerusalem . . . are often used to set forth the church of God in the New Testament dispensation. The church on earth and the church in heaven are in one important sense the same thing, as they constitute but one family" (Eph. 3:15)[2]. The church is the bride of Christ and like a bride should be fair and undefiled. Only the saving power of our Redeemer can cleanse the lives of men and women, redeeming them and making them worthy to be members of the church, the body of Christ, the bride of Christ.

Christ referred to the saved as the church, and often in the New Testament just the word "church" indicates the Christian people. Often however, the fuller designation "church of God" is used.

For nearly three centuries the church was obedient to her God and her mission; her message, her salvation, and her victory swept across much of the known world. Within three hundred years after a cross was raised on Golgotha's hill to crucify an unknown Galilean, the emperor of the Roman Empire bowed in allegiance to the One who had died on that cross. And then came night! Men sought to usurp the power of Christ; a man declared himself the mediator between God and man! Thus arose the organization known as the Roman Catholic Church, and she practically ruled the western religious world for about a thousand years. At various stages during this spiritual night, reformers sought to break from their spiritual bars and restore pure Bible preaching which always produces the church of God, but each time they were either subdued or driven to exile.

In the early sixteenth century the hunger in the breasts of men to worship Christ in biblical freedom intensified, and God in mercy called forth brave and holy men to break the Roman yoke. The great Protestant Reformation of the sixteenth century is a dream story come true, and it thrills the heart of every Protestant. From Martin Luther to this

---

[2]F. G. Smith, in *The Revelation Explained*, p. 303.

day reformers have arisen, heralding what they believed to be Bible truth. Some made themselves heard; others left little impression. Each of those who struck a useful blow for the church did so with a distinct doctrine revealed to him from God's Word.

Martin Luther thundered out his discovery of justification by faith. Roger Williams declared Christ the head of the church and water baptism by immersion the true form of that ordinance. John and Charles Wesley taught repentance, justification, sanctification, and holiness. John Calvin stressed equality of ministerial authority. George Fox urged that men heed the leadings of the Holy Spirit in a society of peace, friendliness, and love. William Otterbein and Martin Boehm emphasized spiritual birth and foot washing. All these reformers preached some Bible truth. Some organized religious groups which came to be designated as churches.

However, Morton, it is not biblical for a church to stress only one or two Bible doctrines. No church can be the Bible church by proclaiming only a smattering of truth. The true church must declare all the Bible truth, as that truth is discovered or revealed, and strive to match the spirit and vigor of the first-century church. The prophet Zechariah said, "At evening time it shall be light" (14:7). That is, in the last days the glorious gospel of God shall encompass the world. All must hear the good news of the gospel. Christ said, "Preach the gospel to every creature."

From the very beginning, the church of God has been the body of Christ, the bride of Christ, the redeemed. The church includes all the truly born-again souls, lovers of truth who accept the Bible as their rule of faith. The church of God includes all who preach all the New Testament and endeavor to practice all of it. It consists of people who are ready to breathe fresh religious air, to preach and practice newly revealed truth, to stretch and strive to match the standard set by the first-century church.

More than eighty years ago Daniel Sidney Warner was a member of a religious group that did not subscribe to the idea that we must walk in and preach new light as it is focused on our pathway by the Holy Spirit. In the Northern Indiana Eldership of the Winebrennerian Churches of God Warner did not find the necessary liberty to preach the whole truth of the New Testament. In 1881 at a meeting of that group at Beaver Dam, Indiana, Warner spoke "of his convictions and declared that he could no longer conscientiously remain a part of their fellowship. In a dramatic moment he asked if there were others who would also take their stand as being free from all sectarian division. Five people stood up. Together they walked out of the meeting—and out of sectism forever. This small group from Beaver Dam became the first congregation of the Church of God."[3]

So, Morton, that was the beginning of the Church of God movement as we know it today. From that small group of five, the movement has grown until now there are thousands of congregations throughout the country, and followers of the Church of God in all parts of the world. Let me hear from you again next week. I shall be ready to answer another of your questions.

Sincerely, your friend,

HILLERY

---

[3]John W. V. Smith, in *Heralds of a Brighter Day*, p. 42.

2

WHY THE CHURCH OF GOD?

Dear Morton:

It was good to receive your second letter. It is most rewarding to discover one so deeply interested in studying about the Bible church. You seem to relish every morsel of truth that you can find. May I urge you to continue your sincere search. Keep reading, studying, praying, and may your heart remain open to the Holy Spirit! You will soon discover that the most thrilling reality is revealed truth from God's Book.

It makes me happy to know that you received "much good" from my answer to your first question, "What is the Church of God and when did it begin?"

Now let's go to your second question, which is most intriguing, "Why the Church of God?" Furthermore, I note that you also ask, "Why not be a minister in a larger, more established group, with many more years of experience, where you would have greater advantage? And why do we need such a distinct movement as the Church of God?"

Morton, we believe the Church of God movement matches the church of the first century most closely. This is true in interpretation and presentation of the doctrines of the Bible, in the practice of Bible unity, and in the requirements for church membership. Of course, I must hasten to assure you

16

that such an assumption is not based on religious conceit or bigotry; after serious search, sincerely I believe this to be true. We do not claim to be a perfect group; yet I believe that God's interpretation of perfection in regard to his church is something entirely different from man's interpretation.

Let me illustrate it this way: A small girl named Judy had a deep love for her mother and a perpetual desire to express her love. One day while her mother was visiting a friend, little Judy, weary of her toys, spied a pillowcase her mother had been hemming and had not completed. Judy finished the hemming, then pressed it as nicely as she could. The mother returned later with a friend and saw the work Judy had done. The hemming was crude and the stitches uneven; the iron had been too hot and had slightly scorched the material. But the mother knew that Judy had done this work, crude as it was, out of a heart of love. Her eyes filled with tears. The work was perfect in that mother's eyes. As long as we seek Bible truth with holy zeal and as long as we strive to practice that truth by the grace of God, God will be pleased and say, "Well done, my child."

The Church of God congregations with general offices at Anderson, Indiana, form a movement within the universal church. It is not a church among churches. If we were only a church among churches, there would be no place for us. While other church groups build high fences or stout creeds around the truth revealed to them, we remain open to the Bible and to the Holy Spirit for new truth, and we share this truth with any and all who desire it.

No one would deny that Christendom is torn by selfish schisms today. Jesus prayed, "That they all may be one; as thou, Father, art in me, and I in thee, that they also may be one in us: that the world may believe that thou hast sent me" (John 17:21). Nevertheless, Christians are divided into more than two hundred religious groups, most of them standing immovable with some truth, but not enough truth. Protestantism is a house divided against itself. Every church body has its peculiar method of church membership, its own form of church government, its distinctive name. This is exactly what the Bible does not teach! The church of God is commissioned to preach and practice unity on a scriptural level and to expose the world to that gospel and practice. Western Christians have grown used to sectarianism; however, it is the highest hurdle to reaching the non-Christian world. Christians are not fulfilling the purposes of the church Christ founded as long as they are divided. The Church of God movement must sow the seeds of Bible unity for which our Lord prayed.

It is true, Morton, that I might have greater advantage, from the world's point of view, ministering in a larger, longer established church group, and yet there is no real gain or glory in conforming to a pattern that one feels to be contrary to God's design for his church, however great the advantage. I feel that my call to the ministry of Christ is not to seek personal aggrandizement but to interpret the Bible correctly and to preach and practice it with all the zeal and intelligence God has entrusted to me.

We believe that our movement has a responsible role to fill in the plan and purpose of God's well-ordered design for the salvation of mankind. When the reformers broke with the Roman church, in our opinion, the break was not wide enough. Some Protestant groups today worship only one step removed from Roman Catholicism. In their revolt against Rome, some groups came much nearer copying the

Roman church than they did the New Testament church. Therefore, in reality, the revolt in many cases did not follow the New Testament pattern but used the Roman Catholic yardstick.

We believe, Morton, that this revolt against a counterfeit church must continue until all schisms are done away with, and the church is established, "a glorious church, not having spot, or wrinkle, or any such thing; . . . holy and without blemish" (Eph. 5:27). For seventy-five years we have taught in the Church of God

the unity of God's people. Things have changed since we first began to teach this. We used to hear men get up in public and argue why they were Baptist or Methodist, etc. They would just about un-christianize those of other faiths. They would fence in the particular truth they held, and would say, "Come to us and get it if you want it." When the pioneer brethren first began to preach unity, they were greatly persecuted and misunderstood. But now almost all outstanding Christian leaders see the evils of denominationalism, of a divided church. Many condemn sectism in stronger terms than we ourselves do. Our teaching has begun to take hold because it is the truth. Men just cannot get around truth; it is on their hands. Truth does not need defending; it needs proclaiming. It will take care of itself.[1]

It is true that many church leaders see the fallacy of denominationalism, and still they do not have the signals straight; they, too, often run the wrong way! From various man-made organizations they seek the answer. But the answer was conceived long ago in the mind of God and is recorded in the Bible. (See Ephesians 4:11-16.) Recently, I had a lengthy discussion with a very dear friend of mine, pastor of a large denominational church. He inquired of me the doctrine of the Church of God. When I explained to him what we teach, he said, "Hillery, you are right!" Yet he hardly knows what to do about setting his house in order.

[1]Warren C. Roark, in *The Church*, pp. 90-91.

We believe that God will keep working on the minds of good men until the true church is seen, loved, and embraced by all Christians.

It would be surprising to many people to know how effective the revolt against sectarianism in church circles is. Especially lay people cannot harmonize a Christendom sliced into more than two hundred segments with the prayer of Christ that his people be one. Millions of honesthearted Christians are revolting against a scheme of man-made church union. Last summer a staff writer for a large newspaper wrote an editorial about the problems of a divided church. He had, during the past two years, visited over one hundred churches of all kinds, including the one where I am pastor. This unbiased writer had many splendid comments to make about various groups, and then he presented a viewpoint we seldom hear anything about—that of the nonchurchgoer.

He stated that sixty-four million, or about 40 per cent, of the people in the United States belong to no church, and he proceeded to give the reasons for nearly one-half of our total population refraining from participating in the American churches. His opinion is that these men and women are not "bad" people, who desire to live a profligate life; neither are they atheistic; nor are they too lazy to get out of bed on Sunday morning. This reporter believes that the underlying cause for all this church shyness can be summed up in one word: "doubt." Many of these people cannot see eye to eye with all the complicated creeds, dogmas, rituals, of organized religion. Most nonchurchgoers have a firm belief in some sort of Higher Power or Force, and they wish to live honorable and decent lives, but they cannot swallow the highly complex church system of our day, says this writer. Then he concludes his editorial by quoting Abraham Lincoln, "When any church will inscribe over its altar as its sole qualification for membership the Saviour's condensed statement of the substance of both the Law and the gospel, 'Thou shalt love the Lord thy God with all thy heart, and with all thy soul, and with all thy strength, and with all thy mind; and thy neighbor as thyself,' that church will I join with all my heart and all my soul."

Now, Morton, I concur with Abraham Lincoln. The Church of God teaches that by the Spirit and the blood of Christ Jesus men are saved, and this is always and everywhere the entrance to the church. People who are actually saved just naturally love the Lord with all their heart, soul, strength, and mind, and their neighbor as themselves. We believe that most people really desire to be members of the Bible church; still nearly one-half of the people of our great land neglect the churches. "We believe that it is possible to set up a congregation so completely void of all organized restrictions that every Christian in the world may be regarded as a potential member thereof without formal act of joining."[2]

Morton, I would not want to leave the impression that the church Christ built was ever completely destroyed or ever became entirely invisible. Some would have us believe that during the dark centuries before Martin Luther's time the true church was wholly invisible. I do not believe that the church of God can be keenly alive in one century, dead the next, and very much alive the next. There was a historical continuity of the visible church; there always will be. The church is divine. Where and when the Bible message is preached and lived, there and then the church exists.

---

[2] C. E. Brown, in *The American Church*, ed. by Ferm, pp. 435-36.

Throughout those centuries before the Reformation the true church found visible expression in the lives of individual Christians both within and without Roman Catholicism. Particularly could devotion and a sense of fellowship akin to the apostolic church be seen in certain minority movements which broke from Roman Catholicism during these long, black years. Dissenting groups such as the Cathari, the Waldensians, and the Lollards dared to stand for their convictions despite persecutions beyond description. Men like John Huss shouted out biblical truth as they understood it even though it led them to martyrs' deaths. Through such as these God's church found expression.

The living germ of God's eternal church had spread in all directions by the sixteenth century, with many religious movements doing their bit in promoting a better understanding of the church and how it serves God's purposes. The Anabaptists did much to champion democratic Christianity and laid the groundwork for religious liberty such as is seen in the United States. In the seventeenth century the Pietistic revival broke out in Holland, Germany, and Switzerland. It was in a Pietist meeting that John Wesley declared, "I felt my heart strangely warmed." He went forth to herald a message of entire sanctification.

So you see, Morton, that the true church of God was ever visible in men who loved the Bible and dared practice its teaching. We believe that the Church of God movement as we know it today has a definite place in God's plan. In this day of religious freedom, we must carry the torch that was lifted high by godly men among the Cathars, the Lollards, the Anabaptists, the Pietists, the followers of Luther and others who made up the reformed church in days when freedom of religion was an unknown commodity. All these truths discovered and preached by the reformers must be bundled together in the message of the true church of God. We are committed to proclaim all "the truth once delivered to the saints"; therefore, we believe we have a definite place in God's plan.

On a hillside about two miles from my home is a huge experimental laboratory for a large chemical company. The prime duty of the workers in this plant is to discover different products that will sell to the public. The church of God is a laboratory of truth; we must never repress our hunger for truth or build walls around the truth we already know. We must build walls around nothing. We are commissioned to declare all the truth revealed to this day and search the Word for more truth to preach. Jesus said, "Go ye . . . teach all nations . . . to observe all things whatsoever I have commanded you" (Matt. 28:19-20). This "laboratory of truth" has been busy.

Our great contribution has been the teaching of the brotherhood of man, the unity of God's people, the nature of the church, the leadership of the Holy Spirit, and the fact of church membership by faith the same as salvation by faith, sanctification by faith, divine healing by faith, and forgiveness of sins by faith. We teach that the church is composed of all believers in Christ everywhere. It takes faith, many times, to see the church made up of fallible men and women. But it is true: "Ye are the body of Christ and members in particular."

We must take all the great truths of historic Christianity which God has revealed to others and add to them the truth which He has unfolded to us, and carry it to the whole wide world. We are not to make a creed of these truths and keep them for ourselves, but we are to share them with all other Christians everywhere, then keep our hearts open for any truth that others may have for us.

We are not to try to bring the whole Christian world to us or to our standard, for we have none. We must try to bring them to *God's revealed* truth which we enjoy that they may share it with us.

When we have done that we will automatically be one. There is unity in the truth of Christ.[3]

I shall be anxiously awaiting your next letter, Morton, and I pray that I shall be able to satisfy you with my answers.

Sincerely, your friend,

HILLERY

[3]Warren C. Roark. in *The Church*, pp. 89-90.

3

WHY THE CHURCH OF GOD? (*Continued*)

Dear Morton:

You are certainly "Johnny-on-the-spot" with your questions! Between each letter I receive from you I live in a perfect dither, wondering what the next question will be, and whether I can answer it properly. You say, "You will never know how much good I am receiving from your answers." Well, I must confess I am gaining knowledge myself as I study to answer your questions.

It strikes me that I need to say more about your second question, "Why the Church of God?" Then we will come to the observation you make in this letter: "I note your remark about the reformers' break with Rome not being wide enough. Would you please be more specific, for I always understood that the reformers made a clean break with the Roman church and that they restored the New Testament church. Where did they fail?" I shall try to point out specific weaknesses in the break with Rome.

When Christ announced his church, he said, "I will build my church; and the gates of hell shall not prevail against it" (Matt. 16:18). He did not say he was going to build three hundred churches or one hundred or twenty or even two churches. He said, "I will build my church."

For a clear-cut picture of the church and a thorough understanding of its function we must return to the first-century church, the church that produced the New Testament. If I were sent out to cut lumber into three-foot pieces, I would not cut one piece and measure the second by the first, the third by the second, and so on. I would measure each piece from the first to the last by the yardstick. Some are too prone to measure the church by the teachings of some reformer of the sixteenth, seventeenth, eighteenth, or nineteenth century. By so doing they have made a bad mess of things. To capture the true meaning of the church of God we need to study the first-century church.

The New Testament affords us a portrait of the morning church and allows us to listen to the voices of those who were in its service. Luke said he wrote his Gospel "that you may fully know the truth of what you have been taught by word of mouth" (Luke 1:4, Weymouth). Luke was there when that early church was converting men by the thousands. He was there when the Christians were persecuted, jailed, beaten, and killed. He was there to give us a correct picture.

It takes all Bible truth combined to produce the true church. The church of God today can be produced only when gospel truth is preached and the believers walk in spiritual light. When we fail to preach and practice all the New Testament, we fall into denominationalism, and man-made creeds become our guide and rule. The church founded by Christ, the church the disciples were part of, was eventually swallowed for the most part by Romanism, because truth was weakened and Christian discipline loosened.

Morton, let me reiterate, we must always measure the church today by the first-century church. When we deviate from the New Testament, we cut loose our moorings and immediately drift into error. The early church "continued steadfastly in the apostles' doctrine" (Acts 2:42). When these early saints met together, they devoted themselves to the instructions given by the apostles. And where did the apostles get their information? They had lived with Christ, listened for long hours to his teachings. They had firsthand information; they were present when he said, "I will build my church, and the gates of hell shall not prevail against it."

What is the apostles' doctrine? The apostles' doctrine is simply what the apostles believed, practiced, and taught. They proclaimed God, the loving Father and Christ the divine Son of God, the only Savior of the world. They preached repentance and conversion. By precept and example they taught water baptism by immersion for all converts to this new faith. They held forth the truth that all born-again Christians are candidates for and should receive the baptism of the Holy Spirit.

They preached the second coming of Christ and the general judgment; with fervor they attested that the wicked will be punished with everlasting fire, whereas the righteous will be rewarded in heaven. They believed, taught, and practiced divine healing, the Lord's Supper and foot washing, and righteous living. They did not take a fragment of truth and isolate it and build a religious organization upon it. They were not satisfied to snatch one brand of truth from God's burning altar and declare that to be the gospel; they proclaimed it all.

Our message today, Morton, must not be less than the message then. It is imperative that we match the gospel of the first-century followers, else we cannot match them in quality of life. The likeness of the church you attend to the church Jesus built can be determined by the truth it receives and practices. Just holding to and proclaiming one truth will never produce the Bible church.

Let us see where the church has failed in keeping the apostles' doctrine. Let us see if the reformers really broke with Rome. The first-century church understood the real method of becoming a Christian. Jesus said, "Repent ye, and believe the gospel" (Mark 1:15). On the first day of the total functioning of the church Peter declared, "Repent, and be baptized every one of you in the name of Jesus Christ for the remission of sins" (Acts 2:38). In the day these words were spoken, the church was young and obedient, and great multitudes were saved. But the nominal church today is far removed from that morning church. People by the millions are joining man-made churches today, and the promoters of this church joining have not one precept from the New Testament to stand on. Jesus said, "Ye must be born again," and later the Apostle Paul said, "Therefore if any man be in Christ, he is a new creature: old things are passed away; behold, all things are become new" (II Cor. 5:17). To Paul, a Christian was one born again, a new creature.

In the denominations today members are added by many and varied methods. Some are baptized by water into the denomination; some are confirmed; some are accepted by shaking the minister's hand; still others are voted in by a committee. Others are considered to be admitted to the church by making a public confession of the Lord Jesus Christ; others enter by subscribing to a creed. However, these are not God's plan. At best, they can only be a substitute for God's divine plan. The apostles of the first century knew nothing of these man-made methods of getting into the church. According to the apostles' doctrine, "The Lord added to the church daily such as should be saved"

(Acts 2:47). Therefore, true church membership is not acquired by some outward ceremony, but by an inward change of heart.

Morton, I think you know without my telling you that church joining has almost completely replaced Christ's plan of rebirth. If it was necessary in the first century for the Lord to add to the church daily such as were saved, it is still imperative today. We do not believe that any religious body can improve on that method. Therefore, the first-century church taught and practiced that men are saved by the new birth, and by that method only God added believers to his church. Man had nothing to do with the adding of members to the first church, and any church group today who adds members by its own authority is not the true church. To be the true church of God in the twentieth century, we must be a fulfillment of the original church that Jesus established. When men accept members into a religious organization they inadvertently include unsaved persons, but when God "adds," be assured he will not make such mistakes. Before the Roman Catholic Church ever began receiving members God was adding to his church. Prior to the organization of the first Protestant church body in the sixteenth century, Christ had been selecting those who were qualified to be members of his body, the church. And God is still capable of doing the adding. Paul said, "Now hath God set the members every one of them in the body, as it hath pleased him" (I Cor. 12:18). Surely God must be displeased at the many methods by which man tries to add members to the church.

The early church continued in the apostles' teaching regarding water baptism. We have no record of their ever baptizing by any other method than immersion. When anyone realizes that water baptism is a witness to the work of salva-

tion wrought in the heart and understands what it really
means, all other modes, such as pouring and sprinkling, must
be ruled out as not biblical. The word "baptize" has been
taken over from the original Greek word, which means to
dip in or under water. Thus there is only one Bible method
for the ordinance of baptism, and that is immersion.

What, then, is the meaning of water baptism? Religious
organizations which believe in sprinkling or pouring tell us
that baptism is a type or symbol of cleansing, and that is certainly right. Yet, as Dr. Brown remarks, "baptism is also
a symbol of our association with Christ in his death and
resurrection, whereby we are raised from sin in this life and
shall be raised from the dead in that august day of His
power." Moreover, baptism symbolizes our union with
Christ. The pages of the New Testament are fraught with
this teaching. "Therefore we are buried with him by baptism into death: that like as Christ was raised up from the
dead by the glory of the Father, even so we also should
walk in newness of life. For if we have been planted
together in the likeness of his death, we shall be also in the
likeness of his resurrection" (Rom. 6:4-5).

Going down into the water is an outward testimony that
the old life is dead and buried, that God has saved us "from
sin," that we have cut off our sinful practices. Coming up
out of the water signifies that we are resurrected from death
in sin and are become new creatures in Jesus Christ. "Therefore if any man be in Christ, he is a new creature: old things
are passed away; behold, all things are become new" (II Cor.
5:17). Coming up out of the water is a public testimony
to the world that we have taken our stand for God and truth
and that we have identified ourselves with the people of God.
However, Morton, Christ's command to baptize (dip) is

being flagrantly disobeyed. Some religious groups let the candidate choose what mode of baptism he will follow. Is it not strange that anyone should interpret the New Testament record thus?

We are told that infants should be baptized, and millions have been. Yet it is interesting to note that infant baptism is first mentioned by Irenaeus, about A.D. 185, long after the Bible writers were dead. Certainly, Christ did not command infant baptism. There is no evidence that the disciples practiced it, nor does the Bible even allude to it. One writer argued in favor of infant baptism from the doctrine of original sin. The great Latin writer, Tertullian, spoke distinctly of the practice but discouraged it, expressing the belief that delay of baptism was desirable until character was formed. He might have said, "Baptism should be delayed until one has knowledge of sin. Then, when he has repented and been converted, he is a candidate for water baptism."

The New Testament church taught and the Bible states, "Repent and be baptized." However, nowhere does the Book infer that a child is guilty of sin; but it does say, "Except ye be converted, and become as little children, ye shall not enter into the kingdom of heaven" (Matt. 18:3). If God holds the child innocent in spite of original sin, who are we mortals to declare him guilty? It is significant that such men as Tertullian held to the innocency of childhood. Yet it is still more significant to note that infant baptism did not become universal until the sixth century, and we know that by the sixth century the Word of God had been perverted by a thousand heresies. You will notice, Morton, that I have written at length on water baptism, because no Bible doctrine has endured more attacks.

The morning church continued in the apostles' teachings

regarding the experience of sanctification. Among many de-nominational groups, the general idea is to oppose, deny, or ridicule the doctrine of sanctification. It takes little discernment, however, to know that millions of sincere Christians need something they do not possess. There are honest people who endure a life of perpetual fear, who are controlled by jealousy, malice, covetousness. They say their prayers, go to church, pay their tithes, but there is no joy in the service of God, no power to live free from guilt.

We believe such people need to let the Holy Spirit of God purge from their lives that old inherited nature of Adam. Paul spoke of the God of peace sanctifying wholly. The Revised Standard Version reads the same way (I Thess. 5:23). Other translations speak of being made holy through and through. How, you ask, is the great work to be executed? The Apostle Paul said, "Being sanctified by the Holy Ghost" (Rom. 15:16). Christ said he would send the Comforter who would be in us to guide us into all truth. At Ephesus, this same Paul asked the Christians, "Have ye received the Holy Ghost since ye believed?" (Acts 19:2).

The first-century church continued in the apostles' doctrine regarding divine healing of the physical body. Christ told the disciples that they should "lay hands on the sick, and they shall recover" (Mark 16:18). The Apostle James wrote, "Is any sick among you? Let him call for the elders of the church; and let them pray over him, anointing him with oil in the name of the Lord: and the prayer of faith shall save the sick, and the Lord shall raise him up" (5:14-15). In spite of this simple, practical teaching, many religious organizations deny this Bible truth. The Church of God believes it and practices it, and many sick and dying people have been completely healed.

Also, the early church continued in the apostles' teachings regarding the Lord's Supper and foot washing; we in the Church of God still practice these ordinances. Some religious groups just practice one and reject the other, and some reject both.

All these apostles' doctrines were practiced, and the church prospered, for two hundred years or longer, and then man thought he could formulate a set of doctrines that would be more effective than the ones designed by the Lord. For over a thousand years the Roman church wrote her own creeds and practices regarding salvation, methods of church membership, water baptism, and so on. When the reformers broke with Rome, they held to many of the Roman Catholic doctrines instead of returning to the New Testament for their directions. In the practice and teaching of some of the doctrines the reformers hardly broke with Rome at all. Certainly they did not make the gap wide enough. The image of Rome shadows many of the doctrines taught by Protestantism today. The Church of God feels that it must teach New Testament truth until all shall know and practice it.

Sincerely, your friend,

HILLERY

4

WHAT DO WE BELIEVE ABOUT CHRISTIAN UNITY?

DEAR MORTON:

Your questions about the doctrines of the Church of God have truly stirred me. Believe me, I am excited! Since you began pouring these questions in, I have uncovered some truths about the Church of God that I was not too familiar with myself. You know, Morton, I sincerely hope some of your hunger for truth rubs off on me. Your letters and questions are throbbing with excitement.

Since your first letter, I have expected the question you ask today: "What does the Church of God teach about unity?" This question is pressed upon every true Christian today. Anywhere sincere followers of Christ gather together you can hear Christian unity discussed.

We in the Church of God have given much thought to this important doctrine; as a matter of fact, our interpretation of Bible unity gave birth to our movement. I shall try briefly to give you an idea of our stand on this all-important subject.

When just a lad I used to watch my mother cut pieces from Father's worn-out trousers. From my outgrown shirt she took the part that was not too badly worn, and from my sister's old apron she found a small piece she could use.

Then she purchased a few yards from a bolt of material which lay on the merchant's shelf. For days she sewed, working together this material from so many sources. When she finished her work, she had a quilt.

The death of Christ is wonderful in many respects. It is wonderful for one thing, in that through his death Christ gathered "in one" the children of God. Like the variegated pieces in a quilt, the children of God have come from many places—from every walk of life, every race and color, every nation. These children of God, through the death and resurrection of Christ, form a new colony, a new nation. They are not joined together like the pieces in a quilt, but they have been "gathered together" and through the great mystery of God's redemptive plan, "knit together in love." Jesus, through his death on the cross, offers every man an experience that will give him a taste of universal brotherhood.

Now, Morton, we know already what some people will say about this; they brand it a foolish dream or a dangerous delusion. They think that diversities of race are insurmountable barriers and insist that we ignore at our peril the differences of color, speech, tradition, and culture. Yet when God speaks, we must act, regardless of previous patterns. Before Jesus' death, Caiaphas, the proud high priest, not realizing what he was saying, prophesied that Christ would "gather together in one the children of God" (John 11:47-52).

Christ prayed earnestly before his death that his followers would be one, that the world might believe (17:21). The plan of God has always been for one church and one gospel that makes us all one. On your daily job you will find men and women eager to talk about religion; yet they are confused, hardly knowing what to believe. One sincere man said to me, "What *can* one believe?" The fact remains that too often New Testament teaching has been scuttled for a man-designed gospel. Man's desire to usurp God and his power was at work even in the first century. Paul wrote the church at Colosse, "Beware lest any man spoil you through philosophy . . . and the tradition of men, after the rudiments of the world, and not after Christ" (2:8).

To me, Morton, the healthiest sign in the church today is the hunger among Christians to be united in one great force for God. And the fact that you do find Christians everywhere with this yearning for the unity of God's people provides a suitable environment for the message of the Church of God. Of course, it is not the actual unity of all believers that men differ so much about as it is the means by which that unity is to be made visible.

All sorts of attempts have been made to bring about solidarity in the human family. The Jews dreamed of Jerusalem as a world metropolis with political and religious authority over all peoples. Assyria, Greece, and Rome sought to control the world and force upon the people political unity. In the early fourth century Constantine tried to use Christianity as a unifying force in his empire. With recognition by the government the church became increasingly popular and gradually lost its early purity and power, as more and more unredeemed persons were accepted as members.

In modern times the efforts to unify the world's peoples continue. Some have tried to do it by force; others by spreading abroad ideas—such as the worship of the state, as in Russia—which they hoped would bring the whole world to one state of mind. We have had the League of Nations and now our United Nations. Poets, prophets, statesmen, have hoped and labored for some common understanding that would bring some sort of unity to the vast chaos of this world.

However, Bible unity cannot be forced, nor can it be brought about by legislation, nor even by agreements. Christian unity can come only to those who are indwelt by the Spirit of Christ and who see that the unity of the Spirit is more important than anything that has separated Christians.

Seventy-five years ago, when the Church of God movement was just beginning, a divided church was considered the ideal, and our people were often severely criticized. Indeed they came in for a great deal of persecution because of their emphasis on unity. Now that most church groups are preaching some sort of unity, our movement likes to feel that it had something to do with bringing this Bible truth to the attention of the religious world and we believe that long strides have been made toward uniting God's people.

On the bottom of the swimming pool in the YMCA in an American city the builders placed a beautiful tile emblem symbolic of the spiritual, mental, and physical nature of man. At the center of the familiar red triangle is the Bible opened at John 17:21. When a boy could not make out the wording, he swam to the bottom and read it. "It says, 'John 17:21,' but what is that?" he asked a man near by. "That they all may be one," the man answered. The boy's reply was prophetic: "You sure have to go through a lot to find that out." Christians have gone through a lot to discover this Bible truth, but the signs are encouraging.

As a matter of fact, many Church of God people believe that an awakening of Christendom has been taking place that may prove second only to the Protestant Reformation. We may not agree with all the mechanics of the ecumenical movement that is sweeping across Protestant and Orthodox

churches; nevertheless we must admit that that movement
has been scaling some high denominational walls to give
the idea of Christian unity a hearing. Also we are glad that
the hearing has often been favorable.

With eyes wide open the Church of God movement views
these evidences of hunger for Christian unity among Christian people everywhere. The ties that bind Protestant groups
together have been strengthened by the formation of the
World Council of Churches. On World Communion Day
many faiths that once stood aloof participate; this enlarges
and enriches the united fellowship. The celebration of the
church's birthday, designated as Pentecost, helps to create
understanding and brings to a focus the obligation of all
Christians toward the world's underprivileged. The common
ground of our religious heritage is highlighted in the Protestant Reformation Day observances.

The recent ecumenical conference held at Evanston, Il-
linois, evidenced a sharp desire among churchmen, both laymen and ministers, for a workable Christian unity. This
history-making conference was attended by representatives
of some 160 faiths from 47 countries. At such meetings
Christian men exchange ideas, and many barriers to Christian
unity melt away. The National Council of Churches, together
with the local and state councils, has done a great deal toward
bringing various church groups together, both laymen and
the ministry, for Christian service.

It is not unusual to find the churches of a city or neigh-
borhood co-operating in rehabilitation programs for delin-
quent youth and on behalf of refugees. This uncovers the
united concern for human needs. Many Protestant and Orthodox churches have banded together to keep church and
civic charity programs free from gambling—bingo, for in-

stance. Such action is a stout builder of higher ethics on a united level. Many national radio and television programs are demonstrating the *likenesses* of religious groups rather than their differences. For instance, the Church of God's Christian Brotherhood Hour, with W. Dale Oldham, preacher, is aired on scores of stations in the United States and more than a dozen stations in other countries. This program is sowing seeds for a "united church for a divided world." I have talked with men of other church groups, many of whom praise the biblical soundness and the evangelistic appeal of this broadcast.

For three-fourths of a century the Church of God movement has been pioneering in the effort to restore Bible unity. The ancient church fathers thought of schism as the gravest of sins. "Nothing angers God so much as the division of the church," wrote Chrysostom. "Even if we have done ten thousand good deeds, those of us who cut up the fullness of the church will be punished no less than those who cut up his body" (referring to the crucifixion). Augustine felt the same way: "There is no just necessity for dividing the church; schism surpasses all crime."

Charles Lamb was once asked by a friend if he was musical. He answered, "Sentimentally, I am disposed to harmony, but organically I am incapable of a tune." When one studies the attitude of ecclesiastical bodies, he thinks of Lamb's response. Sentimentally they are disposed to harmony, but organically they are incapable of achieving unity. However, Morton, I feel that Christians are moving up and in from a merely sentimental attitude to something substantial. The castle in the sky is getting a firmer foundation. The Church of God agrees with the ancient Church Fathers that schisms are sinful, and it has charted a course and program to lead men to this age-long goal of the human soul—the unity of God's people.

Having said all this about the favorable trends toward Christian unity, I must reveal the other side. Dr. Peter Ainslie, outstanding apostle of Christian unity of his generation, wrote a book with the title, *The Scandal of Christianity.* From his book comes this power-packed paragraph:

Half of Christendom is not on speaking terms with the other half, separated by superstitions, ignorance, and fear. Whatever else this condition may reveal, it certainly is not Christian. But the denominationalist consoles himself that these conditions are matters of conscience, oblivious to the fact that Christian conscience has been bred largely in the hothouse of an unhealthy and biased theology.

Since Dr. Ainslie wrote his book, much has been said about division being the "scandal of Christendom," and may I add my testimony to that truth. One sometimes hears of church scandals involving a preacher running off with the deacon's wife or the treasurer escaping with the church money, but as far as the church is concerned, the number one scandal of the twentieth century is its 250 divisions—its witness pierced by 250 divisions! Still each existing denomination hangs on for dear life, as though its particular interpretation or emphasis is more vital than the unity of all the people of God.

An old legend tells about a herd of mules that was attacked nightly by a pack of hungry wolves from a near-by forest. When the wolves came, the mules began kicking viciously in all directions. Consequently the mules maimed and injured each other while the agile wolves escaped unharmed. Finally, a wise old mule called the rest together for a conference and made known his plan. That night the wolves came yelping from the forest as usual but instead of the mules kicking promiscuously, they all put their heads together in a circle and began kicking outward. The wolves were put to flight, and the mules did no harm to each other. Christian people need to get their heads together right now, quit kicking, and study and pray for the true method of Christian unity.

Each church group gathers behind its four walls on Sunday and sings, "We are not divided, all one body we," but until Christendom gets together in heart, head, and hand, those words should be reshuffled and sung, "We are all divided, not one body we." Divided churches produce divided communities, divided communities produce divided states, and where it stops no one knows.

An outstanding churchman said the other day, "If the united church could arise out of the denominations, I would be the first person to respond. But I do not see it on the horizon. The denominational leadership is lacking the courage and the vital Christianity it will take to lead out in such a movement."

This may be true, yet in a crisis courage and vital Christianity have a way of becoming visible. The world is worn out, tired of war; men want peace. Christendom is tottering from many schisms, and her sincere Christian leaders yearn for unity; they are tired of countering the Bible. This is a day of crisis! On February 3, 1943, at 1:15 A.M., the Army transport *Dorchester* was torpedoed and sank within twenty-five minutes in iceberg waters near Greenland. Four chaplains were on board, a Roman Catholic, a Jew, and two Protestants. When there were not enough life belts to go around, they took off their own and gave them away. When last seen, the four men of God were standing arm in arm praying. As they went to their death united in the service of their common Lord, so the church should stand together, unitedly, fighting evil and serving a dying world. I am sure these four men thought little at that hour of crisis of their particular brands of religion—they thought about God! The church must draw closer to God and seek to interpret his will and plan for all men.

The fact that the church once possessed unity is known by most followers of Christ, and some of them desire restoration of that unity at almost any cost. I believe the flame in their hearts will be fanned to a roaring blaze, and millions of born-again Christians will rise up and demand a working unity of all believers.

Now, Morton, I do not wish to "throw a wet blanket" on anyone's interest in anything that may lead us toward religious solidarity in Christ Jesus. If God's people want the right thing long enough they will eventually seek the right method to secure it. And yet I know that the true way to restore Christian unity is to seek a closer fellowship with the Master, Christ Jesus. The first disciples were joined together; they loved one another; they were kind to one another because they were drawn to Him. Increased faith and hope in Christ will bring about a sincere search among God's people for unity.

I am extremely anxious, Morton, for you to know where I am seeking to place the emphasis regarding unity. If we seek unity without first understanding our directions, we only add more obstacles to our already existing frustrations. It is not uniformity that we seek; we seek unity. The road to uniformity may lead to force or to an imposing organization, or as one dubbed it, to "a mere amalgamation of differences." There is a tremendous difference between uniformity and unity. When the Roman Catholic speaks of the oneness of the church, he has in mind uniformity, which is something external, an outward pattern.

When the reformers broke with the Roman church, in many cases, they clung to the Catholic pattern of church organization. But when the true disciple of Christ speaks of the oneness of the church he is thinking of something deeper than the surface, an experience of the heart and spirit. True Christian unity is not predicated on, nor is it dependent upon, institutions, but upon Christian experience. The unity which the Church of God seeks comes *not* through techniques, regulations, theories, and institutions, but through a childlike trust in our Lord Jesus Christ and self-surrender to the Holy Spirit. That kind of unity, and that kind only, will be acceptable and workable.

I recall reading the account of an American writer as he described a scene on the deck of the battleship *Missouri,* where General MacArthur was speaking as Japan surrendered. Though he had the power to threaten and destroy Japan, he spoke not of war, but of peace. Said MacArthur, "We have had our last chance. . . . If we do not devise some greater and more equitable system, Armageddon will be at our door. The problem basically is theological and involves a spiritual recrudescence and improvement of human character." Then, in deliberate tones, the General concluded: "It must be of the spirit if we are to save the flesh." In my opinion, that is the way to unity, "of the spirit." The way to unity is by learning the way of Christ, by praying for spiritual guidance, by practicing the laws of Christ, which are love, service, and sacrifice. Only through that method will the people of God ever have a consciousness of the kinship of Christians everywhere that is deeper than differences.

Quickly, Morton, I will state three pertinent facts about how Christian unity can be restored and close this letter. First, Paul said, "By one Spirit are we all baptized into one body [the church]" (I Cor. 12:13). The fact that every born-again Christian does possess the Spirit of Christ furnishes us a sound beginning for unity. Second, Paul also said that God sets the members every one of them in the body as it pleases him. No provision is made for division. God rules division out! Third, every one of the members fills the place in the body that God has designed he should. The members of the church of God being divinely arranged will function according to the divine plan and will divinely constitute the church that Jesus built, the church of God. This is the unity the Church of God movement seeks.

It affords me a great deal of pleasure that my answers in last week's letter, as you say, greatly helped you. I shall be awaiting your fifth question.

Sincerely, your friend,

HILLERY

5

ONCE A MEMBER ALWAYS A MEMBER?

DEAR MORTON:

From your letter today I see that your appetite for truth has not been dulled; yet I do sense that you are somewhat disturbed. May I encourage you, Morton, by the fact that often we make our most effective search when we are disturbed. Just do not let your disturbance turn to depression.

While I expected you eventually to ask the question that you present today, I did not have any idea it would come so early in your Christian experience! You say, "There are many Christians on my job at the plant, and their conversation confuses instead of enlightening me." You explain: "One person says that all people will eventually be saved; another sets forth the idea that only the 'elect' can be saved, and the 'elect' can never backslide. Still another says that all may be saved, and if they do backslide, they can be saved again." It is not difficult to see, Morton, why you are confused.

I notice that you also ask: "What does the Church of God teach about the eternal security of the soul? The people I work with talk about it so much." Please be patient; study hard and keep your mind open to God. He will help you understand everything you wish to know about his church.

Often lay people discuss what they hear their ministers

45

preach on Sunday. The questions you present regarding salvation have theological labels, and each originates from a religious pattern developed over the years. A certain doctrine widely held in religious circles is referred to by different names—predestination, eternal security, final perseverance of the saints, and once in grace always in grace. Many fine Christians have never taken time to investigate this teaching for themselves; they have simply let their ministers interpret theology for them. Often Christians, discussing such subjects, come to extreme interpretations and confusing answers. The theology of the religious world is triangular in design. By that I simply mean that most people who profess Christianity hold to one of three major schools of thought regarding Christ's atonement. These three have reached the masses as Universalism, Calvinism, and Arminianism. As simply as I possibly can, I shall seek to explain these three approaches to the Christian doctrine of salvation and show which the Church of God embraces and why.

The Universalists stand at one point of the religious triangle. Origen, one of the Church Fathers (A.D. 185-254), was the principal early exponent of Universalism in Christian circles. His doctrine of a temporary punishment of the wicked paved the way for the Roman Catholic doctrine of purgatory. That is, there may be a short period in which man will suffer for his sins, but in the end he will be fully redeemed. They tell us that the death of Christ on the cross will eventually save every man.

Matthew's Gospel records Christ's description of the final judgment day for all peoples. He very plainly shows two groups of people at this judgment scene, the saved and the lost. He says to the saved: "Come, ye blessed of my Father, inherit the kingdom prepared for you from the foundation of the world" (25:34). To the lost he says: "Depart from me, ye cursed, into everlasting fire, prepared for the devil and his angels" (vs. 41). Now the Universalist would have a difficult time explaining away those words of Christ Jesus.

I recall your mention that these folks use Hebrews 2:9 to prove that all will be saved: "Jesus . . . by the grace of God should taste death for every man." It is true that Christ did die for every man. I think Dr. Charles E. Brown [1] very ably explains this:

Let us say that in a certain district there is a factory which must be reached by a roundabout road for people coming from the west, because it is cut off by the grounds of a large estate. Finally, the owner of the factory goes to the administrators of the estate and buys a public right of way through the grounds of that estate so as to make easy access to his factory. In due time this road is opened up to the general public. Now those who have been driving around another way may drive through this new road. However, there is no compulsion about using this new road. The philanthropist has not merely bought the right for so many thousand people to use the road; he has bought the right for all travelers to use the road. Nevertheless, he will get no refund if not all travelers use the road. There is nothing compulsory about it. It is simply an offer freely made to those who will freely choose. That is the way of the atonement and of redemption in Christ. It is not that the way is opened for a limited number of millions of people; it is open for all. Nevertheless, those who do not choose to use the road are not entitled to any refund for not using it; neither is there compulsion on anybody to use it. This seems to me to illustrate the universality of the way of salvation opened by the atoning death of Christ. It is a gift offered to all men, but only those who accept the gift receive the benefit.

From another point of the triangle comes the Calvinistic theology which insists that the atonement provides salvation for only the select, the chosen. This theory says that in the infinite mind of God, ages before Calvary, a limited number of people were predestinated to be included in the atonement.

---

[1] In *Questions and Answers*, pp. 86-87.

Nothing is more impossible than for any of this chosen group to resist the call, and it matters not how far they may stray into sin, they cannot be lost. However, Morton, the word "predestination," interpreted in such limited scope as this runs counter to God's salvation plan. The Church of God movement rejects entirely the terrible view that certain people in the world are the elect, and the rest are to be damned irrespective of their own longing for salvation. The Church of God loves the catholicity of the New Testament invitation: "The Spirit and the bride say, Come. And let him that heareth say, Come. And let him that is athirst, come. And whosoever will, let him take the water of life freely" (Rev. 22:17). Someone has well said, "The elect man is whosoever will; the damned man is whosoever won't."

At the third point of the triangle we find another school of thought known as Arminianism. This doctrine presents a teaching that harmonizes with the thought and pulse of God that we discover in the Bible. In brief, Arminianism says, "Christ died on the cross, finishing the plan of redemption that will completely save all who will accept it. The conditions for salvation are the same for every man—repentance toward God, faith in his Son, and unreserved obedience to God's commands."

Much could be said about all three of these schools of thought, and I shall have more on the subject of Arminianism before I close this letter. For the moment, let us lay aside Universalism and Arminianism and focus our attention upon Calvinism, the purveyor of the doctrine of eternal security. That is your chief concern now.

The famed Church Father, Justin Martyr (100?-165) wrote, "I hold . . . that such as have confessed and known the man to be Christ, yet have gone back . . . and have denied that this man is Christ, and have repented not before death, shall by no means be saved," thus agreeing with the writer of Hebrews (10:26-30). An early consideration of this teaching is found in the writings of a devout Catholic monk by the name of Augustine, who was born in the fourth century.

Some of the leading exponents of the doctrine of eternal security say, "It is nowhere taught that any part of salvation depends upon the faithfulness of man." If this were true, some might not see any reason to live a clean, sober, moral life. The Apostle Paul evidently felt that faithfulness was a decisive factor in our salvation: "Teaching us that, denying ungodliness and worldly lusts, we should live soberly, righteously, and godly, in this present world" (Titus 2:12). Thus, Morton, it is clear that our salvation does depend upon our actively rejecting what is unlike God and embracing wholeheartedly what is of God.

A teacher of the doctrine of eternal security writes, "I have no doubt, though some may disagree with me, that Ananias and Sapphira were saved people . . . when death came to them from the hand of God. I believe they went directly to heaven." Such an interpretation has a strange ring when we read the actual Bible account. Peter said, "Ananias, why hath Satan filled thine heart to lie to the Holy Ghost?" (Acts 5:3). Luke tells us that after the hand of the Lord had smitten both Ananias and Sapphira, "great fear came upon all the church." Now, Morton, you know as well as I do that great fear would not have come upon the church because two people had been taken to heaven. I believe this "great fear" was a result of the church's witnessing two lying, backslidden hypocrites struck dead by the hand of almighty God.

Morton, the Church of God neither teaches nor believes the doctrine of eternal security, because the Bible does not teach it. Just the other day a fine Christian woman said to me, "I was terribly shocked to learn that one of my sisters, who was recently converted, feels that she can stray far from Christian principles, and still be safe. She says that after you are once saved, you cannot possibly fall." That sort of teaching makes the devil laugh and the imps chuckle, for it leads men astray from God.

One of the most godly men who ever graced this world was John Wesley. His ministry completely changed the course of Great Britain. His constant prayer was that through the grace and care of Christ he should never fall, backslide, and be lost. He put poetic expression to the thought of millions when he wrote:

> *Ah, Lord, with trembling I confess*
> *A gracious soul may fall from grace;*
>
> . . . .
>
> *Lest that my fearful case should be,*
> *Each moment knit my soul to Thee.*
> *And lead me to the mount above*
> *Through the low vale of human love.*

For scriptural basis, the eternal security people often use these words of Christ's: "I give unto them eternal life; and they shall never perish, neither shall any man pluck them out of my hand" (John 10:28). But concerning whom was Christ speaking? By reading verse 27, we may learn. "My sheep hear my voice, and I know them, and they follow me." Christ was speaking about his followers—not about liars, hypocrites, backsliders. The writer of Revelation puts it this way: "Be thou faithful unto death, and I will give

thee a crown of life" (2:10). Every disciple of Christ must
bear this grave responsibility of being faithful, and that
faithfulness must be unto death.

Paul addressed the church of God at Rome as those "called
to be saints" (1:7), and to the Corinthians he wrote, "Do
ye not know that the saints shall judge the world?" (I Cor.
6:2). By judging the world, Paul simply meant that the
Christian standard is the criterion by which the whole world
will be judged. But what right would one who is a liar,
hypocrite, and a cheat, though he bear the name of Christ,
have to sit in judgment on the world? None whatever.
While those who teach the doctrine of eternal security tell
us it is impossible for a Christian to backslide, yet the
Bible not only tells us that man can lose the grace of God,
but it gives example after example of those who did
backslide.

If you search your Bible, Morton, you will see that our
first parents, Adam and Eve, backslid. God told them, "Of
the tree of the knowledge of good and evil, thou shalt not
eat of it: for in the day that thou eatest thereof thou shalt
surely die" (Gen. 2:17). But like the eternal security people
today, they reasoned that man cannot live free from sin; they
did not believe that God meant what he said. So they ate
the forbidden fruit, died spiritually, and were expelled from
the garden.

Paul charged the Galatians, "Ye are fallen from grace"
(5:4). John flung the same charge at some: "Remember
therefore from whence thou art fallen, and repent, and do
the first works" (Rev. 2:5). It would be impossible for one
to fall from a housetop until he first got up there. This is
equally true in religion. It is impossible to fall from grace
until we have first attained that holy estate. These who had

been Christians were accused by the apostles of being "fallen from grace" and were told to repent.

The doctrine of eternal security is a theory of man and not a doctrine of the Bible. Nowhere does the Bible infer that any of the New Testament writers were tainted with this teaching. Jesus warned against listening to the precepts of men and told the false teachers of his day that they were "teaching for doctrines the commandments of men" (Matt. 15:9).

This "once in grace always in grace" theory is not new. Paul wrestled with it when he faced the heathen philosophies of his day. Its complexion has changed with the passing of the centuries, yet its central theme is the same. Paul's refutation was this: "Let every one that nameth the name of Christ depart from iniquity" (II Tim. 2:19). For those who wish to know who will have eternal security, let God answer, through the Apostle John, "He that doeth the will of God abideth forever" (I John 2:17). As long as the children of God do the will of God they are secure and no one can snatch them out of the Father's hand (John 10:29); however, no one is forced to remain in the Father's hand. Eternal security comes only to those who *accept* the grace of God and *abide* in it.

The doctrine of predestination has split the Christian world into debating groups for many ages. While we do not think that any given individual is predestinated to salvation or despair, we do believe that God purposed to have a holy church from the beginning of all time. The existence of the church is predestinated, though the question of our membership therein is left open to our own free choice to accept or reject.[2]

That is our position as far as predestination is concerned. Morton, I wish to close this letter by stating that the

---

[2]C. E. Brown, in *The Church Beyond Division*, p. 77.

Church of God movement embraces the Arminian approach to the freedom of man's will, because we believe it to be the correct interpretation of the New Testament; this we believe is the New Testament position. A prominent Protestant scholar (1560-1609), by the name of Jacob Arminius, returned to the original tradition of the New Testament. Arminius taught that one may be saved from sin here and now. This doctrine was later accepted and developed further by the Wesleys, the founders of Methodism.

Against the Calvinist theory that Christ died for the elect only, Arminianism asserts that He died for all, though none except believers receive the benefits of his death. Man is not totally depraved and therefore can co-operate with God in spiritual regeneration. Calvinism holds to the doctrine of the total depravity of man. Whereas the Calvinists teach "once in grace, always in grace" Arminius emphasized the possibility of a lapse from grace. We accept the Arminian approach to these issues because it squares with the New Testament.

With the greatest of eagerness, Morton, I await your next question!

Sincerely, your friend,

HILLERY

6

HOW DO CHURCH OF GOD PEOPLE LIVE?

DEAR MORTON:

You will, perhaps, never know how happy I am that my answer to your question on eternal security of the soul helped lift you from a state of confusion on the subject. I rejoice that you can say, "I am going in high gear for God again."

It is thrilling also to note that you say, "I simply love to read the Bible and I check all Scripture references in your answers." It is good that you check these references; it will help acquaint you with the Bible.

However, I think the greatest joy that came to me from your last letter was to have you say, "I have been attending services at the Burgville Church of God, and what they teach there just *sounds* right." Morton, the truth always sounds right to God's children; moreover, truth is food to the Christian's soul.

It is only natural, I suppose, that your most recent question should be: "How do Church of God people live? Do they commit sin? Can we be free from sin in this life? Some of the fellows where I work say that all Christians sin and will continue to sin as long as they live in the world, and they ask forgiveness every day." Well, Morton, it is going to afford me much pleasure to seek to answer this question.

Recently, the findings of a United States Senate committee

54

revealed some strange facts regarding Russia and her treaty agreement. In the last twenty-two years they (the Russian leaders) have made fifty-two major agreements with the West, and have broken fifty of them. This may be understood in the light of a remark by Joseph Stalin, "Words must have no relation to actions—otherwise, what kind of diplomacy is it? Words are one thing, actions another. Good words are a mask for concealment of bad deeds. Sincere diplomacy is no more possible than dry water or wooden iron."

Morton, people who talk about being saved by the blood of Christ and yet fail to harmonize their acts with their profession should have little trouble understanding Stalin. Jesus said, "This people draweth nigh unto me with their mouth, and honoreth me with their lips; but their heart is far from me. But in vain they do worship me, teaching for doctrines the commandments of men" (Matt. 15:8-9). In place of letting the New Testament be the measure by which all Christians live, some of the Protestant reformers formulated their own standards. All downward steps taken by the early church were caused by men who dared substitute their theories and creeds for the word of God.

Harnack, in his *History of Dogma,* very clearly points out this downward trend:

An empirical conception of the church was created in which the idea of a holy life in the Spirit could no longer be the ruling one. . . . She [the church] became a condition of salvation; but the result was that she ceased to be a pure communion of the saved and of saints. . . . It was quite a logical proceeding when about the same year 220 Calixtus, a Roman bishop, started the theory that there must be wheat and tares in the catholic church and that the Ark of Noah with its clean and unclean beasts was her type.

Therefore, we can rightfully conclude that the idea that

Christians sin was retained by some of the reformers from the teachings of the Roman Catholic Church.

For this cause, we must go beyond the Roman church; we must not stop with the Protestant Reformation. Our religious liberties will be cramped by sectarian concepts until we return to the New Testament interpretation of God's church. The angel who introduced the redemption plan said, "And she [Mary] shall bring forth a son, and thou shalt call his name Jesus: for he shall save his people from their sins" (Matt. 1:21). This lovely theme permeates the entire New Testament from Matthew to Revelation: "He that is righteous, let him be righteous still: and he that is holy, let him be holy still" (22:11).

Morton, I do not desire to encourage controversy, for we have had too much of that in the church already; nevertheless, I feel that anyone has the right to state his convictions on any given subject. The argument in the Arminian-Calvinistic controversy waxed hot. The Arminians labeled the Calvinists, "Once in grace, always in grace—no matter how disgraceful you may be." The Calvinists fired back in double-barreled style, "Saved today and lost tomorrow—and often a dozen times in between." However, such mud slinging is detrimental to all, though, of course, sincere Christians on both sides are seeking to do the will of God.

The Church of God believes its people should live a redeemed life. For one to say he accepts Christ is not enough, for a sinner is an alien, an enemy, a rebel, and therefore exposed to the wrath of almighty God. The first business of the unsaved is to repent; I mean he must undergo a thoroughgoing repentance. Redemption comes only to those whose repentance goes deep. "Repentance toward God" includes restitution. The lost can approach the saving Christ only through repentance, motivated by godly sorrow for sin. Such repentance clears the way for the soul to plead for mercy, cast its sinful self in humble contrition upon God, and believe his Word, trust him for Jesus' sake to cancel the past and make him a child of God, a Christian.

When the Lord cancels the sinner's past, and claims him as his child, the believer becomes a new creature and lives like it (II Cor. 5:17). Someone has said, "A genuine Christian ought to be as distinguishable amongst his fellows as a civilized man amongst savages; and what will make him so will be something he has got from Jesus Christ, and which he could not possibly have got elsewhere." That is the way Church of God people live!

The Apostle Paul, who wrote one-fourth of the New Testament, was a positive exponent of righteous living. He wrote, "This is a faithful saying, and worthy of all acceptation, that Christ Jesus came into the world to save sinners" (I Tim. 1:15). Remember, Morton, "to save" means "to deliver," in this case from sin and its consequences. And John wrote, "No one who is a child of God commits sin. A divine germ remains in him, and he cannot sin—because he is a child of God. By this are distinguished God's children and the devil's children: no one who fails to act righteously is a child of God" (I John 3:9-10, Weymouth).

Christ Jesus, the teacher of the disciples, said, "I am . . . come . . . to call . . . sinners to repentance" (Matt. 9:13). Morton, I should like to say this much about repentance: it means to get a new mind, heart, and spirit, and it produces the fruit of righteousness. Luke wrote, "To give knowledge of salvation unto his people by the remission of their sins" (1:77). The fact that our sins have been remitted (forgiven) assures us that we are saved. The Church of God believes that the gospel does something for people *here* and *now*. People need help now; they need deliverance from sin now. The gospel that Christ entrusts to his church will dispel the darkness, his blood will cleanse the heart, his Spirit will lead into victorious Christian living now. We can be free from sin now.

One day in the office of a friend whose business is politics I noticed a motto hanging on the wall. It read, "If you can't beat them, join them!" We realize that the exponents of "sinning religion" mislead many good people, and we know we cannot convince everyone that the Bible clearly teaches that all Christians ought to live righteously. However, that fact does not justify our joining them.

Many who think they have to sin are honest about it. They have heard the preaching of that theory so long that they do not know what the Bible teaches. Large church groups have proclaimed this erroneous doctrine so long that a false pattern has been established, and the masses follow that pattern rather than search the Scriptures for themselves. "As men cease to be holy themselves they begin to turn earnest attention to holy things. Since by universal consent there were believed to be no holy people, men sought connection with the Eternal through holy things and places."* Thus, we hear much about holy water, holy bones, holy vestments, but, Morton, nothing must ever eclipse the holiness of man's heart. Only holy men can constitute the church of God. We admit that Martin Luther made great gains in pulling away from Catholicism; yet, he lost so very much when he denied that any living person could be free from sin.

Morton, you say that some of the men with whom you work confess their sins every day. Nowhere in the Bible do

*C. E. Brown, *The Apostolic Church*, p. 234.

we have such teaching. A guilty soul may repeat his confession again and again, yet he has only repetition, not remission—only a consciousness of sin, not cleansing from sin.
What every human heart needs is not remembrance of sin,
but removal of it. Christ, and he alone, actually gives us this
removal. By him "we have redemption through his blood;
the forgiveness of sins, according to the riches of his grace"
(Eph. 1:7).

R. A. Torrey tells of a man, who, although soundly converted when just a boy, grew up and fell into the bondage
of strong drink. In despair he came to Dr. Torrey to find
help. He learned, to his surprise, that he had only believed
half of the gospel. He had indeed trusted the Christ who
"died for our sins according to the scripture." In the crucifixion of Christ he had found pardon, peace, and joy. But
he knew nothing of the other half of Christ's gospel, "that
he rose again the third day according to the scriptures."
There and then the poor victim knelt and trusted the risen
Savior to free him from his awful bondage to drink. When
Dr. Torrey next met him, the man cried, "It works!" The
truth of the risen Christ sets men free indeed.

On the cross Christ died to bring pardon for past sins,
and on Easter morn, when Christ rose from the grave, deliverance from the power of present sin was made available
to anyone who will receive it. Christ is able "to save them
to the uttermost that come unto God by him, seeing he ever
liveth to make intercession for them" (Heb. 7:25).

Church of God people teach and live a sanctified life, a life
empowered by the Holy Spirit of God. The object of sanctification is a holy church. "Husbands, love your wives, even
as Christ also loved the church, and gave himself up for it;
that he might sanctify it, having cleansed it by the washing

of water with the word, that he might present the church to himself a glorious church, not having spot or wrinkle or any such thing; but that it should be holy and without blemish" (Eph. 5:25, ASV).

You will notice, Morton, that the Scriptures affirm that by the act of sanctification the church is to be "glorious . . . not having spot or wrinkle . . . or any such thing . . . but . . . holy." Now, the church is the saved people; consequently, we believe that the members of the church must be holy. The words "holiness" and "sanctification" have caused more conflict in religious circles than almost any other words you can mention. The reason for this is that some groups who identify themselves as holiness people have some weird interpretations of righteousness and have preached some fantastic ideas about Christian living. Still others have set up such a high standard that no one can possibly reach it. Thus the words "holiness" and "sanctification" have become frightening.

Why does God want a sanctified church? Paul said the reason is that it might be holy. Isaiah also declares for holiness: "It shall come to pass, that he that is left in Zion . . . shall be called holy, even everyone that is written among the living in Jerusalem: when the Lord shall have washed away the filth of the daughters of Zion, and shall have purged the blood of Jerusalem from the midst thereof by the spirit of judgment, and by the spirit of burning" (4:3-4). Even today God wants the "spirit of judgment" against all unholiness and wrong. Inconsistent conduct cannot be tolerated in God's church if it is to enjoy God's blessings. The "spirit of burning" means the Holy Spirit. John the Baptist said, "I indeed baptize you in water unto repentance: but he that cometh after me is mightier than I; . . . he shall baptize you in the Holy Spirit and in fire" (Matt. 3:11-12, ASV).

In preaching on the subject of holiness it is possible to have plenty of law but little "spirit," because it is so easy to direct the message wholly to externals, whereas the "spirit of burning" should always pierce the heart. We need more Pentecostal fires that will burn sin out of the church. You recall the case of Ananias and Sapphira in the Jerusalem church. After the "spirit of burning" was applied to these two sinning Christians, believers were the more added to the Lord, multitudes both of men and women. When Christian leaders get the correct interpretation of sanctification and holiness and present this truth kindly and intelligently, Christians will find unity, and men and women are going to be saved.

Perhaps, Morton, you have already heard some say, "My church does not believe in holiness." If so, you might answer, "If the Bible has any meaning, your church must then be an unholy church, and it is certainly the wrong one, for Paul said that Christ gave himself that his church might be holy." Others say, "I do not believe in holiness." Such people are destined to miss heaven, for the Bible tells us that without holiness no man shall see the Lord (Heb. 12:14).

God wills that the church be sanctified, that it may be presented to Christ without "spot, or wrinkle, or any such thing," that it may be a glorious church. Sanctification produces both unity and glory in the church today, "that they may be one . . . that the world may know that thou hast sent me" (John 17:22-23). "They were all filled with the Holy Ghost . . . and the multitude of them that believed were of one heart" (Acts 4:31-32). Church of God people live the sanctified life.

Morton, this experience of sanctification is purely an individual matter. The responsibility is yours and mine. Christ spoke to the disciples in these terms, "Blessed are those who hunger and thirst for righteousness, for they shall be completely satisfied" (Matt. 5:6, Weymouth). All sincere Christians feel the need of God's Spirit. Christ said that we who hunger and thirst for the Spirit of righteousness, if we seek him, shall be "completely satisfied." The unsanctified individual feels the lack of spiritual power. He is aware of a foreign element that destroys the joy of Christian living. That foreign element is carnality, and it manifests itself in many forms: envy, pride, coveteousness, love of praise, stubbornness, bitterness, self-exaltation, resentment.

I am confident, Morton, that millions of sincere Christians who are struggling to live for God and finding the going rough, would fully surrender to God if they knew the Bible truth on the subject. They would then experience victory and joy in their Christian lives. God tells us that the Holy Spirit does the sanctifying. Paul in Romans 15:16 speaks of being sanctified by the Holy Ghost. And hear Peter: "God . . . giving them the Holy Ghost, even as he did unto us . . . purifying their hearts by faith" (Acts 15:8-9). This divine work that the Bible calls sanctification purifies the heart, the seat of the affections.

The whole economy of God is based on holiness, and Christians assume the responsibility, by the grace of God, to live that kind of life. Christ said, "Ye shall receive power, after that the Holy Ghost is come upon you" (Acts 1:8). The Holy Spirit empowers every individual to function properly in the place God puts him. When God's people learn that we are placed in the church by a divine act of God's Spirit ("Now hath God set the members every one of them in the body") and that we are able to remain in that body and execute our work by the help of the Holy Spirit ("Ye shall receive power after that the Holy Ghost is come upon you"), then God's people will have learned the secret of true Christian living, and will have little trouble getting together.

True Christians live a redeemed life, a sanctified life, and also a victorious life. Victorious living characterized the first Christians; they were a joyous and victorious group. In the third century, Cyprian became a Christian. He wrote a letter to his friend, Donatus, in which he explained his reasons. The substance of the letter is as follows:

Donatus, this is a cheerful world indeed as I see it from my fair garden under the shadow of my vines. But if I could ascend some high mountain and look out over the wide lands, you know very well what I should see: brigands on the highways, pirates on the seas, armies fighting, cities burning, in the amphitheaters men murdering to please applauding crowds, selfishness and cruelty and despair under all roofs. It is a bad world, Donatus, an incredibly bad world. But I have discovered in the midst of it, a quiet and holy people who have learned a great secret. They have found a joy which is a thousand times better than any of the pleasures of our sinful life. They are desposed and persecuted, but they care not: they are masters of their souls. They have overcome the world. These people, Donatus, are the Christians—and I am one of them.

That is the way true Christians live.

Members of God's church do not believe their energies should be expended *trying to be Christian,* but rather they let God make them Christians and then they do the will of God. "Christianity does not consist in abstaining from doing things no gentleman would think of doing, but in doing things that are unlikely to occur to anyone who is not in touch with the Spirit of Christ." Jesus said, "Whosoever will save his life shall lose it; but whosoever shall lose his life for my sake and the gospel's, the same shall save it" (Mark 8:35). A victorious life, Morton, is a daring life, a dangerous life, in which one at times feels he is about to be rubbed out; yet in the end victory is assured, eternal life is guaranteed.

Paul said that Christians "live soberly, righteously, and godly in this present world" (Titus 2:12). Much courage is needed to live that way in any century, especially in our century. But when God's people are pressed, despised, and persecuted, their Christian witness becomes even more effective. A converted Hindu woman suffered much persecution from her husband. When asked by the missionary what she did when her husband became angry, she said: "Well, sir, I cook his food better; when he complains, I sweep the floor cleaner; and when he speaks unkindly, I answer him mildly. I try, sir, to show him that when I became a Christian I became a better wife and a better mother."

Church of God people accept their marching orders from the Lord: "I am the light of the world. . . . Ye are the light of the world." "Be of good cheer; I have overcome the world." "And they overcame him by the blood of the Lamb, and by the word of their testimony." This profound hope is vindicated in Paul's testimony: "I have fought a good fight, I have finished my course, I have kept the faith: henceforth there is laid up for me a crown of righteousness, which the Lord, the righteous judge, shall give me at that day: and not to me only, but unto all them also that love his appearing" (II Tim. 4:7-8). That is the way Christians live. It is my sincere hope that through this letter, Morton, all your questions concerning how Church of God people live have been answered. It is with a great deal of eagerness that I look forward to your next letter.

Sincerely, your friend,

HILLERY

7

HOW IS THE CHURCH OF GOD ORGANIZED?

DEAR MORTON:

A powerful snowstorm is raging across our state today, and as I read your last letter, occasionally I glanced out at the huge snowflakes that were making the earth pure white. Just as God is the giver of this snow, so he gives us truth to make our hearts and spirits "white as snow."

Honestly, Morton, nothing has afforded me so much solid pleasure and joy as has our study of the church together. Every letter I receive from you bears the stamp of one sincerely searching for knowledge of God and his church. I trust you will never weary in the search.

One does not have to ask whether you are reading. Your questions indicate that you read hours daily. Let us get to your latest question: "I gather from our correspondence that the Church of God is not a denomination, that is, organized like other church groups. Yet, I notice that you have national, state, and local boards. Your weekly bulletin states this. Could you make clear the distinction between the Church of God and other groups? I mean the difference in organization. Please make this simple, for I shall have to explain it to some of the fellows who work with me."

Centuries before the birth of Christ, the Old Testament

prophet Isaiah, speaking of the Messiah to come, said, "The government shall be upon his shoulder" (9:6). Christ declared, "I will build my church" (Matt. 16:18). Later, Paul wrote of Christ, "He is the head of the body, the church . . . that in all things he might have the pre-eminence" (Col. 1:18). The church of God belongs to Christ; he is its head; its organization is upon his shoulders.

The general nature of church government was, therefore, a theocracy. Christ was king and lawgiver, governor and administrator. His rule was a moral and spiritual dominion. It was only when the living, vital union of Christ with his church was lost to view that men began endeavoring to strengthen the bonds of external union by unscriptural human organization and human authority. In the primitive church both organization and governmental authority proceeded from Christ through the operation of the Holy Spirit.[1]

Morton, such church organization finds its validity in the Holy Scriptures. Paul wrote, "God set the members every one of them in the body as it pleased him" (I Cor. 12:18). Luke records, "The Holy Ghost hath made you overseers" (Acts 20:28). Paul's letter to the Ephesians greatly supplements this truth. Christ "gave some, apostles; and some, prophets; and some, evangelists; and some, pastors and teachers, for the perfecting of the saints, for the work of the ministry, for the edifying of the body of Christ" (4:11-12).

Therefore, the Church of God movement takes the position that church organization is for the church people, the redeemed. Nevertheless, much of the church organization of our land is not God rule, but man rule. Some present-day church leaders declare that the church should not be thought of as the camp of the saints, but rather as a community of sinners. However, if the church is a "community of sinners,"

F. G. Smith, in *What the Bible Teaches*, p. 174, Fifteenth Edition.

or if even one sinner were a member of the church, the body of Christ, it would never accept the law, or organization of God. The Bible specifically says, "Be not unequally yoked together with unbelievers" (II Cor. 6:14).

With the apostasy of the church, also came the perversion of the government and organization of the church. After the death of all the apostles, those who had labored with them and had seen God's plan of organization in action sought to continue receiving their directions from God, but soon man began usurping God's place as head of the church. No longer were spiritual qualities necessary for those who filled important places in the church. This was the beginning of a godless ecclesiastical monarchy that disregarded the God-given rights of men. Theocracy was changed to hierarchy, and with this big stick Rome ruled the religious world for a thousand years. We believe that the divine organization of the church was lost during this period.

In I Chronicles 13:9-10, we read about a man named Uzzah who for his impulsive effort to save the ark was struck dead. "When they came to the threshing floor of Chidon, Uzzah put out his hand to hold the ark, for the oxen stumbled, and the anger of the Lord was kindled against Uzzah; and he smote him because he put forth his hand to the ark; and he died there before the Lord" (RSV). Uzzah saw the oxen staggering, the cart shaking, the ark rolling, and he reached to steady it.

The ark of God contained "the golden pot that had manna, and Aaron's rod that budded, and the tablets of the covenant" (Heb. 9:4). The pot of manna was a memorial of the manna upon which Israel fed in the wilderness. Aaron's rod that budded was a symbol that the priesthood belonged to the tribe of Levi. The tablets of stone were the tablets on which the Ten Commandments were written. This precious ark can be likened to the church. And, Morton, when man decides that he must put forth his hand to steady the church, by organizing the church according to his shallow thinking, then what was the true church ceases to be the church at all.

The most powerful human ecclesiastical government known in history was the government of the Papacy of the Middle Ages. It seemed to subdue all under its jurisdiction, but eventually it failed, too. The innate craving for liberty in the souls of men who were crushed and oppressed eventually led them to break out of their bondage and the result was the sixteenth century Reformation. We do not want that kind of government.[2]

The Reformation sought to restore true church government under the Holy Spirit of God. Many reformers rejected entirely Rome's hierarchy, but as I have pointed out to you before, Morton, the breach they made with Rome was not wide enough. They made the mistake of

perpetuating ecclesiasticism by organizing their followers into human systems. In their forms of organization they may not have copied the absolute monarchy, as did the Church of Rome before them, but they copied the other forms of political organizations—the oligarchy, the republic, or the pure democracy—all of which are alike in that they are human, and the authority conferred by them is positional, not charismatic, in character. These humanly constructed systems have divided the ecclesiastical world into many sects, and to this extent they stand in the way of the realization of our Lord's prayer that his disciples might all be one.[3]

You see, Morton, to reject merely Rome's monarchal form of organization was not enough. The church organization of Protestantism can be just as unscriptural as that of the church of Rome. True church organization must find its foundation

---

[2]From "The Government of God," by K. Y. Plank, in *The Church,* compiled by W. C. Roark.

[3]From "The Church of God Reformation Movement," by F. G. Smith, in *The Church.*

in the New Testament. The right church government is a combination of the divine and the human working together in harmony. We reject forms of organization that leave no room for the operation of the Holy Spirit, and we return to the New Testament for all rules and regulations of God's people. Man rule may suffice in a congregation of sinners, but never in the camp of the saints, for Christians are the body of Chirst.

The humble reader of the Bible can readily see the plan of God to organize and govern his people, the church. When Christ said, "Upon this rock I will build my church" (Matt. 16:18), he did not say, "I will build a half-dozen churches, or even two churches." Furthermore, he said nothing about creating a half-dozen forms of church organization or even two different styles of government. In the creation of man, God put about 210 bones in the body. In the body of the normal man, all these bones function smoothly under one head. If man possessed two heads, there would be a constant war between them, for both would, probably, desire to rule at the same time. In the organization of the church, the body of Christ, "God set the members every one of them in the body, as it hath pleased him" (I Cor. 12:18). Christ is head of all Christians, and they are workers together under Him. This means that the church can be organized only under the direction of the Spirit of God. Christ built only one church and designed only one government for the church.

No doubt, Morton, you realize that we live in a day which finds every field of endeavor highly organized, and to the modern mind it would seem paradoxical to have an organization without proper officers to make it function. That has been cared for in God's design of the church also. I like to think of God as the president, Jesus Christ the general manager, the Holy Spirit as the executive secretary. Christ said, "No man can come to me, except the Father which hath sent me draw him" (John 6:44). When Peter preached his great Pentecost sermon men "were pricked in their hearts" (Acts 2:37). That was the Holy Spirit working. Later when Peter was proclaiming Christ, he said, "There is none other name under heaven given among men whereby we must be saved" (4:12). God draws, the Holy Spirit convicts, and Jesus Christ saves. No plan of organization worked out by men can offer such cohesive power as does the Bible plan. The Church of God embraces that plan. Any other system is simply humanity tinkering with divine arrangements.

Early in Old Testament days, men decided to dismiss God and build a short cut to heaven in the form of a tower (Gen. 11). The biggest sin of every generation has been that of leaving God out or of seeking to take his place. Independence, self-sufficiency, and an arrogant spirit have been the downfall of many generations and civilizations. When those people long ago endeavored to build a tower to heaven, they assumed God's prerogatives. This making ourselves self-appointed gods has too often crept into the church, in the form of man trying to organize the church, the body of Christ.

God wants man to keep his puny hands off God's work. You remember that Aaron's sons were struck dead because they took common fire, not divinely kindled, into the tabernacle (Lev. 9:24—10:2). Uzziah, the king, intruded into the ministry without a call from God and was struck with leprosy. Some in their impatience and pride have got ahead of God; they reached their feeble hands to steady the church, with their various forms of organization and government.

They thought changes ought to be made in governing the church, and in place of waiting on God, they assumed his responsibility, and that always ends in serious trouble. The Bible tells us to "wait on the Lord."

In my opinion, Morton, spiritual pride has caused some people to meddle with the divine church. They considered themselves so spiritual that they could not endure others in the same church group, and so they pulled away and formed a church after their own design and organizational pattern. Such spiritual pride has produced more cyclones within Christendom than anything else. It has often affected ministers of the gospel and caused them to organize on dictatorial bases. But God called no one to organize his church; he took care of that.

It is because humanity tries to usurp the authority of divinity that what we call Christendom in the United States is divided into some 250 segments. The walls that divide God's people and hinder the unity of all Christians have been built of the work, theories, governments, and organizations of men who felt they must protect the church. Many honest religious leaders see this mistake now and are projecting their new-found human cures for division. If it is wrong to have some 250 different groups in the Christian church, amalgamation will do little good until the dividing walls have been torn down. If all religious groups will accept the New Testament, the problem is solved.

The early pioneers of the Church of God made a mistake that some pioneers of other religious groups have made in the past: They concluded that since the church of God is the body of Christ, organized, ruled, and directed by the Holy Spirit, no organization within the church could have Bible sanction or be blessed by the Lord. Therefore, they traveled a rugged path, refusing to organize committees and boards to carry on the church work. The ministers were few in number, and most of them were traveling evangelists. Entering a new community they would bring together a group of people hungry for Bible truth. When the ministers left that community, however, the folks who had been gathered together were often soon scattered, simply because they lacked proper organization to carry on the work of the church.

It is my firm belief that God gave these rugged pioneers of the Church of God guidance, and helped them to rightly interpret the Bible on the lines of over-all church organization. To them the church was truly the body of Christ, the earthly habitation of the Godhead. They believed the Holy Spirit could find expression in every truly born-again child of God, and that proper gifts would be imparted to various members as these gifts were needed to govern the church and propagate its doctrines. This is known as charismatic government, or government by the Holy Spirit through the individual members of the church.

Here, Morton, is the difference between the organization of the Church of God movement and that of other religious groups. The church, the body of Christ, can never be organized. God organized the church and set the members in it to please himself. However, it is necessary that the *work of the church* be organized so that it may be effective. While the New Testament nowhere sanctions man's tinkering with the spiritual body of Christ, his church, yet it does show that the early church delegated responsibility to individuals or groups.

Certainly Christ believed in co-operation in Kingdom building, for "he called unto him the twelve, and began to send them forth by two and two; and gave them power"

(Mark 6:7). Luke records, "The Lord appointed other seventy also, and sent them two and two before his face into every city and place, whither he himself would come" (Luke 10:1). This was organization of the work of evangelism; yet this was not an attempt to organize the spiritual church, the body of Christ. "The Lord added to the church daily such as should be saved" (Acts 2:47). In many church groups today the organization includes adding church members to the group. This the Church of God rejects, for such practice is nowhere found in the Scriptures.

To have one church where all Christians may fellowship one another and worship God as Jesus says we must, "in spirit and in truth," there must be one common entrance to that church and one divine government to guide it. If one group catechizes people into its fellowship, another baptizes them into its fold, another has a committee to vote them in, another admits only those who have been born again, how could true Christian fellowship exist among such heterogeneous groups? And how could they all function under divine rule? Any mode of admission to the Christian church other than the new birth (John 3:3) is as foreign to God and the Bible as Holy Spirit inspiration is to Webster's dictionary. When all church people enter the church by the new birth, then there will be no need for any organization except that which is set forth in the New Testament. Just as Uzzah put forth his hand to steady the ark, so modern man has tried to formulate the government of God's church. Such efforts have never had lasting success and never will. Let us never forget that God said, "The government shall be upon his [Christ's] shoulder."

The history of stubborn Israel's experiences on the way from Egypt to Canaan is a classic example of what happens when men think they know more than God. Time and again, Israel took the situation out of God's hands, and every time they ran head on into failure.

The New Testament reveals that the church at Jerusalem ordained seven deacons (Acts 6). Paul organized finance committees to gather relief funds for the poor saints in Judea.

The simple, democratic organization of the work of the Church of God follows the example of the early church as recorded in the New Testament. When their failure to organize the work of the church was seen to be a hindrance, our pioneers sought the Lord and the Scripture for guidance. They discovered that organization was necessary if the gospel message was to reach around the world; thus, children's work, youth work, Sunday schools, were organized that the children and youth might receive proper instruction in religion.

Of course, our first organization as far as boards are concerned was the Gospel Trumpet Company (now Warner Press), which is located in Anderson, Indiana. Its editor soon realized its great strength in getting literature out to the people. Millions of tracts, booklets, books, pieces of church-school literature, papers for children and youth, have gone from its presses to encircle the earth with Bible truth. For over seventy-five years it has printed the *Gospel Trumpet* (in 1962 this became *Vital Christianity*), read by over one hundred thousand people weekly. You can readily see, Morton, that without organization of the church work, we could never have been an effective witness for the Bible truth.

In 1917, the General Ministerial Assembly of the Church of God was organized at Anderson, Indiana, where it convenes each year. The various officers and committees of the General Ministerial Assembly are elected by the Assembly itself; they also elect the various boards for other agencies of the Church of God. In other words, the General Ministerial Assembly has the final word in the work of the Church of God. Even the Warner Press, after having pioneered the field of church-work organization, realized the necessity of surrendering its autonomy to the General Ministerial Assembly so that there would be no independent boards or groups within the church.

Much honor should go to the leaders and organizers of Warner Press, for it was from this board that most of our other agencies stemmed. Among these are Anderson College, our very excellent school at Anderson, Indiana, and the Missionary Board, formed to propagate the gospel around the world. A Church Extension and Home Missions Board was elected to encourage church building and to carry forward the work of home missions. The World Service Committee was organized to co-ordinate the promotion and solicitation of all boards, to promote all the general causes throughout the churches, to distribute funds to all boards in accordance with the approved budget, and to educate in stewardship and church finance.

Other agencies such as the Board of Christian Education, the Board of Pensions, and Christian Brotherhood Hour were organized to give the church a stouter witness to the unchurched around the world and to strengthen our own local works. The national boards have set the pattern for many state and local boards. However, this is what I would have you remember, Morton: Though the movement has organized all these boards that it might do better work for God, no attempt has ever been made to organize the church itself. We leave the creation of the church, the calling of its ministers, the admitting of new members to almighty God.

As far as one's station in the church is concerned, we believe this must be determined by the individual's gifts and qualifications, which he receives from God.

Therefore, Morton, we do not claim to be a denomination among denominations, a church among churches. The Church of God is "a movement within the universal church, an unsectarian movement designed of God ultimately to affect the entire church and bring it to the realization of the grand scriptural idea."[4]

We believe that any religious group that toys with the structure of the church that Jesus built cannot be the true church of God; it is only a human system called "church" but is not really the church. We believe that hierarchies, apostolic successions, priestly corporations, ecclesiastical organizations, and human creeds of any kind are antiscriptural and tend to obscure the church, the body of Christ. We believe that individual obedience to Christ alone, and not to some human creed, is the road to unity of all God's people. We believe that if all religious groups will adopt the New Testament alone for their organizational plan, the sectarian walls that separate God's people will tumble.

Morton, we must never try to control the church, to run the kingdom of God, to direct the organization and government of God. We are not suffering from a dearth of organizers—our drought comes from another cause. We need a fresh touch of God's holy fire to purify, humble, and make us obedient to his divine law. The story is told of a large ship endeavoring to enter port on a stormy night. The bright lights on the hill were clear, but the lower lights had gone out. Unable to see these very necessary lower lights, the captain could not make a safe landing, and the ship crashed on

---

[4]*The Church,* p. 81.

the rocks. The Son of God is the bright light on the high cliff. He is always on the job. True Christians are the little lights along the shore. May we ever be in our place, conforming to the divine plan, shining always, for many ships are lost at sea.

This is enough for today, Morton. Let me hear from you again soon. I am anxious to know what your next question will be.

Sincerely, your friend,

HILLERY

8

WHAT IS THE HIGHEST AUTHORITY IN THE CHURCH OF GOD?

DEAR MORTON:

You encourage me when you write, "Your last letter explaining the organization and government of the church surely makes sense." If we can rightly interpret the Bible, it always makes sense. For every "muddy" answer, there must necessarily be a "muddy" interpretation. The Bible is the most sensible book on earth. I am also happy that you are, as you say, "seeing the light" on many things pertaining to the church of God and that your insights harmonize with the Scripture.

Your question, just received this morning, I suppose follows a natural sequence: "If God has organized the church, and its government is upon the shoulders of Christ, then, what is the final authority in the Church of God? Do you have a Church of God manual or creed book? I understand that various church groups have set up certain norms that contain their creeds, dogmas, and disciplines. Does the Church of God have such? If not, what is the highest authority?"

In the original church the highest authority was the revealed will of God, and the highest authority in the church now remains God's will as revealed in the Bible. For example, Morton, the Bible assures us that there is only one manner of membership in the church, and that is by spiritual birth. Christ sets forth this truth: "Verily, verily, I say unto thee, Except a man be born again, he cannot see the kingdom of God" (John 3:3). Also, notice that "Jesus began to preach, and to say, Repent" (Matt. 4:17). On the Day of Pentecost, Peter proclaimed Christ's gospel of repentance and three thousand were saved. The preaching of Christ's word produced that first church, and the church produced the New Testament, its own acts being set down therein. Therefore, the Word and the church are almost inseparable.

Many have sought to substitute some other authority for that of the Bible in the church. Some would be guided by history, philosophy, creeds, councils, confessions, dogmas, synods. Doubtless much good has come from some of these; nevertheless, the church of God is fresh, clean, and alive and cannot be crystallized into hard and fast rules and creeds of men. The Church of God movement gives no high place to any such things; the Word of God is the Church of God manual and its highest authority. We give free sway to the Word of God when it speaks and that is final.

Throughout the Bible are many passages that vindicate its authority. I shall mention a few: With the Old Testament in mind, Paul wrote: "All scripture is given by inspiration of God, and is profitable for doctrine, for reproof, for correction, for instruction in righteousness" (II Tim. 3:16). And referring to the Scriptures, Jesus said, "They . . . testify of me" (John 5:39). No one could doubt Paul's authority, for he said, "I have received from the Lord that which I also delivered unto you" (I Cor. 11:23). Christ Jesus upholds the authority of the Word by saying, "He who . . . does not receive my sayings has a judge; the word that I have spoken will be his judge on the last day. For I have not spoken on my own authority; the Father who sent me has himself given me commandment what to say and what to speak" (John 12:48-49, RSV). The Bible is the Word of God, hence the first and last authority in the church of God. The pioneers of our movement

did not profess to originate any new doctrine or truth. Many of the doctrines which they preached had been preached by others. This fact has caused undiscerning persons to suppose that one doctrine was appropriated by the pioneers from one denomination, another doctrine from another denomination, and thus was built up a composite, synthetic, eclectic system of teachings which was in no sense unique. But such was not the view of our pioneers.[1]

Those who have made any study of the Church of God at all know that our pioneers were committed to the proclamation of all the truth contained in the Bible. They were not guided by what others thought or taught. Says Dr. Gray, "They accepted the Bible as their sole authority and sought the illumination of the Spirit for interpreting and preaching it." Just as the Word of God was the rule, guide, and authority of our early pioneers, it so remains in the Church of God to this day. Christ said, "I have given them thy word" (John 17:14), and the Church of God believes that word to be all-inclusive and sufficient. Disciplines, creeds, rules, and regulations of men often arise from unscriptural interpretations and become an insult to God. No one has been able to improve upon the Word of God.

Creeds, dogmas, and the rest are often agents to help man understand the plan of God, but more often they tend to crystallize into hard and fast rules that bind men instead of allowing the Spirit free play. For example, the Nicene Creed,

---

[1]From "The Legacy of Our Pioneers," by A. F. Gray, in the *Gospel Trumpet*, January 7, 1956.

which dates back to A.D. 325, put a formal end to the violent dispute that raged regarding the Trinity, and the Apostles' Creed serves as a measuring stick of doctrine and orthodoxy among almost all Christians. These in a way are good. On the other hand, back in the seventeenth century there arose an ecclesiastical creed declaring that some are destined to serve God, and when once converted they cannot possibly miss heaven. This gave birth to the "once in grace always in grace" theory. Also this creed set forth that those who are not destined to inhabit heaven are predestinated to be lost, and they can do nothing about it.

Now, Morton, you can see how hurtful such creeds can become to Christendom. This doctrine of predestination, though it has lost much of its "punch" over the past three hundred years, is still a stumbling block to many sincere people. It depicts God as an unfair tyrant, who consigns many people to hell fire and carries his few pets to eternal bliss. Nowhere does the Bible teach such. This is purely a man-made creed. Why not accept the Bible on the subject? It says, "Whosoever will, let him come."

Creeds may serve as useful guides along the Christian way, like maps, pointing out for the pilgrim both pitfalls and high ground. Yet all over the world you can find millions of people laboring under the galling yoke of creedalism. A few years ago, I made it my business to inquire among the people of Rome, Barcelona, and Paris as to their concept of religion. The answers given ran something like this: "Our church is bogged down in creeds. It has become a commercial octopus drawing all the financial blood from our veins and giving little in return. We are tired of it."

Now this heavy creedalism is a deadly danger in that it implies that all truth has been explored and exhausted, a kind of we-have-arrived attitude. This sort of creedalism says to the searchers for truth, "You are a heretic if you dare think otherwise." The reformers rejected such systems; however, they set up religious booths and began business next door. Some of their creeds, a few years after their break with Roman Catholicism, grew teeth and claws that sent many people to their graves because they refused to conform. In such cases, one wonders which is the more vicious, the parent or the child.

The Jews had their religion in old wineskins of creeds, dogmas, and laws, that could not hold Christ's new wine of love and spiritual freedom. The stoutly constructed creeds of Protestantism must be replaced by the divinely inspired Word of God before God's people can get together in one church, in one purpose. Only through the authority of the Word of God can the twentieth-century church match the vigor of the first-century apostolic pattern. And, Morton, I have the fondest hope that more Christians in all religious groups will soon see the imperativeness of returning to the Bible for final instructions and authority. That day may be nearer than we think.

In many ways our day is much like Jesus' time. Millions are still seeking their spiritual living water from the broken cisterns of worn-out creeds. Powerful Bible truth has been revealed and proclaimed, but the philosophy and traditions of men have been so threaded through this truth that it has become as clouds without water. When man seeks to "nail down" his interpretations of truth, damming the free course of truth, he usually is found with a mixture of error and truth. A parable may illustrate this fact: The devil and one of his favorite imps were walking along. They saw a man coming toward them, and just as they neared him, he reached

up and plucked a large piece of truth from the thin air.
This scared the imp, and he said to his master, "Sir, did
you see that? Are you not afraid for him to have that truth?"
The devil replied, "No, I am not frightened, for when man
gets truth, he names it, organizes it, dogmatizes it, and then
crystallizes it into a creed, and then it is not truth at all."
I do believe, Morton, that creeds have a way of eliminating
Bible truth and accepting as almost final the thoughts of men.

The word "creed" is derived from the Latin word *credo*
which literally means, "I believe." A creed is a system of
beliefs held to be vital in religion. The bundle of creeds
within Christendom has become a tremendous load for
Christians; I have personally talked with those who groan
under their weight. Down through the years, men have interpreted God's Word and will, and their interpretations, false
or true, have become creeds that guide themselves and others.
As I stated before, some creeds are good, some not so good;
nevertheless, if the church should be totally governed by the
many creeds of men, the Spirit of God would depart from
Christendom, for the church cannot progress under purely
human dictation.

The main textbook of the church must ever be the Bible,
for only the Word of God gives life. "The word of God is
full of life and power" (Heb. 4:12, Weymouth). It is not
difficult to find those who get their direction from the creed
of their particular denomination rather than from the Word
of God. Those who depend upon creeds will find it hard to
be sensitive to the guidance of the Word; they have already
had the final revelation, as far as they are concerned. Who
would dare say that man has already received all the truth
that God wishes to reveal to him? The psalmist cried, "Thy
word have I hid in mine heart, that I might not sin against

thee. . . . Thy word hath quickened me. . . . Thy word is a lamp unto my feet, and a light unto my path" (119:11, 50, 105). In this case the psalmist used the word "quickened" to mean restoration of the spiritual life. Only the Word of God can do that.

It would seem a bit ludicrous for one to pray, "My creed I have hid in my heart that I might not sin against thee. . . . My creed hath quickened me. . . . My creed is a lamp unto my feet, and a light unto my path!" Perhaps no one has ever prayed such an absurd prayer; yet many have thought it. In every age new life, zeal, and power have been injected into the Christian church by pioneering souls who have refused to conform to the crystallized creeds of men. The Roman church, walled in by dogmas, creeds, councils, claimed to be the only Christian church, and branded all other religious groups as schismatic and heretical.

Luther, Calvin, Zwingli, and the other reformers would not accept the Roman theory. These men threw a biblical punch that staggered Rome. Every sincere Christian is thankful for the bold step these men made toward getting back to the true church and the correct interpretation of the Word; on the other hand, I must repeat that these reformers did not pull entirely away from some of the mistaken practices of Rome. Council followed council, conference followed conference, confession followed confession, and though these newly formed dogmas and creeds took on shapes different from Rome, they were in many cases departures from the inspired Word.

In the nineteenth century came D. S. Warner, whose purpose was to restore the apostolic church, with the Bible as center and authority. Warner contended that the Bible was given by the Lord before creeds came from the minds of men, and of course he was right. In place of crystallizing part of the Word into an iron-clad creed, Warner preached that God's Word is living and is the final hope of the world. I believe that, too, Morton. Warner took for his postulate the words of Paul: "All scripture is given by inspiration of God, and is profitable for doctrine, for reproof, for correction, for instruction in righteousness: that the man of God may be perfect, throughly furnished unto all good works" (II Tim. 3:16-17).

Not only did Paul and other Bible writers affirm this truth, but "every Christian scholar in the world knows that it was also the teaching of the Jews concerning the Old Testament before Christ's time, and during the days of Christ and of the apostolic church. Every such scholar also knows that this was the traditional teaching of all Christian believers and of all the creeds of Christendom until modern times."[2] Human ignorance and bias find their way into the creeds of man, but the Bible is the Word of God.

I am aware, Morton, that argument for creeds, dogmas, and such, is often based on the fact that parts of the Bible seem to form a creed. The contention is that the Ten Commandments are a creed, the Lord's Prayer is a creed, the first article of our faith was a creed: "I delivered unto you first of all that which I also received, how that Christ died for our sins according to the scriptures; and that he was buried, and that he rose again the third day according to the scriptures" (I Cor. 15:3-4). However, there is a great difference between a creed divinely inspired and recorded in our Bible, and a creed designed by human thinking and containing only bits of the Word of God. All Christian scholars accept creeds found within the Bible as valid and divine; only some

[2]C. E. Brown, in *Questions and Answers*, p. 35.

men will accept creeds written by man. I cannot stretch my mind far enough to harmonize the two.

George Calixtus, of the late sixteenth and early seventeenth centuries, a Lutheran professor, sought to promote mutual denominational forbearance by giving a high place to three ancient symbols, or creeds: the Apostolic, Nicene, and Athanasian creeds, which he believed contained the essentials of Christianity, but his efforts were chilled by a cold reception. His hearers and opponents accused him of underestimating the accomplishments of one particular reformer. The Church of God does not seek "mutual denominational forbearance," by accepting one creed and rejecting another. We contend that when the Bible is preached, believed, and embraced as the final authority in the church, creeds of men will fade away, and the membership of the church will be truly Christian.

We believe the Bible is the inspired and authoritative word of God; the Bible assumes everywhere that it is a message given directly by almighty God himself as the final voice in the church. No organization, or organism, can operate successfully for long if it has several authorities, voices, bosses. There must be a final decision somewhere. In the body of Christ, which is the church, this ultimate authority must ever be the Bible.

Therefore, Morton, our manual is the Bible in general and the New Testament in particular—all in all the highest authority in the movement. All the creeds, dogmas, and disciplines needed by man may be discovered in this great Book. If men knew the contents of the Bible and would declare them, they would have little time to concoct their own philosophies and name them Christian creeds.

The Bible contains the mind of God, the state of man, the way of salvation, the doom of sinners, and the happiness of believers. Its doctrines are holy, its precepts are binding, its histories are true, and its decisions are immutable. Read it to be wise, believe it to be safe, and practice it to be holy. It contains light to direct you, food to support you, and comfort to cheer you. It is the traveler's map, the pilgrim's staff, the pilot's compass, the soldier's sword, and the Christian's character. Here paradise is restored, heaven opened, and the gates of hell disclosed. Christ is its grand object, our good its design, and the glory of God its end. It should fill the memory, rule the heart, and guide the feet. It is a mine of wealth, a paradise of glory, and a river of pleasure. It is given you in life, will be opened in the judgment, and will be remembered forever. It involves the highest responsibilities, will reward the greatest labor, and will condemn all who trifle with its sacred contents.

The unknown author of this quotation had certainly explored and experienced the Word of God. More wonderful still, Morton, is to know that God's Word is open to every humble saint of God. Christ said, "I will build my church, and the gates of hell shall not prevail against it," and to govern that church, he said, "I have given them thy Word" (John 17:14).

Now, let me quickly state some specific areas where the Word is the authority in the Church of God movement: The mode of entrance into the church is by the new birth (John 3:3) ; we accept no other method. Baptism is by immersion only, according to the Word. "We are buried with him by baptism into death" (Rom. 6:4). The government of the Church of God is charismatic, or God-controlled; its members, God-placed (I Cor. 12:18). Our interpretation of sin is biblical: "All have sinned, and come short of the glory of God"; however, we believe that all may be saved if they so choose (Rev. 22:17). Living free from guilt and sin is our discipline, as set forth in the Word: "For the grace of God that bringeth salvation hath appeared to all men, teaching us that, denying ungodliness and worldly lusts, we should live soberly, righteously, and godly, in this present world" (Titus 2:11-12). The name "Church of God" also comes from the Word of God (I Cor. 1:1; II Cor. 1:2). When all God's people adhere to God's Word and his plan, unity will be a natural thing, and the prayer of our Christ, "That they may be one," will be answered.

Let me hear from you again soon, Morton. Please feel free to ask any question you care to. I shall do my best to answer it.

Sincerely,
HILLERY

9

HOW BECOME A MEMBER OF THE CHURCH OF GOD?

DEAR MORTON:

In every question that I have received from you, I have felt the urgency of your inquiring spirit. I have never known one so eager to know the Bible truth about the church. However, your present question is the most urgent of them all; surely, God will never allow such a sincere person to be misguided.

It is good that you have been attending the Church of God more than ever, and I love your humble spirit that motivated you to say, "I want to become a member of the Church of God. I have not asked the pastor yet how I may become a member, for I felt that I could approach you easier than I could him." Further you state, "I attended a church one Sunday morning recently, and the pastor said he was opening the door to the church and inviting all who wished to join. About a dozen children, youth, and adults joined, but all they did was shake the minister's hand and answer some questions, and then they were told they were members of the church. I have heard that some groups vote their members into the church; however, my heart rebelled, for I just did not feel that to be the way to become a member of the Bible church. I work with one of the men who joined the church that morning, and I find that his life is not changed in one single area. He still tells his filthy stories and curses as he did before. I can see no sign whatever of what I believe a true church member should be. Maybe I am judging.

"Now, Hillery, your answers have satisfied me, for you have answered simply and reasonably. Please do not fumble this question, for I am eager to know how I may become a member of the Church of God."

Morton, I have never wanted to be so right in answering a question; may God give me guidance! I am reminded of the last words of Mercutio, the friend of Romeo in Shakespeare's *Romeo and Juliet*. He is wounded in a street fight, and when he is asked about his wound, he says: " 'Tis not so deep as a well, not so wide as a church door, but it is enough, it will serve." It is apparent that Shakespeare was right in many instances; a church door was one of the widest things that he could think of. One of the mysteries of the church is that Christ describes its door as both narrow ("Strait is the gate, and narrow the way that leadeth into life") and wide ("Come unto me, all ye that labor and are heavy laden, and I will give you rest"). Paul declares, "There is neither Greek nor Jew, circumcision nor uncircumcision, Barbarian, Scythian, bond nor free: but Christ is all, and in all" (Col. 3:11).

The poet also has beautifully expressed how wide the door to the church:

> *There's a wideness in God's mercy*
> *Like the wideness of the sea.*

Morton, when we meet Bible conditions, when any person finds the key, the door to the church swings open wide. And what is the key? Once King David backslid and desired much to be redeemed again, and he prayed to God: "Thou desirest not sacrifice; else would I give it: thou delightest not in burnt offering. The sacrifices of God are a broken spirit: a broken and contrite heart, O God, thou wilt not despise" (Ps. 51:16-17). On another occasion he wrote, "The Lord . . . saveth such as be of a contrite spirit" (34:18).

On the Day of Pentecost, after Peter's convicting sermon, thousands were of a broken heart and a contrite spirit, and they cried, "Men and brethren, what shall we do?" And here Peter proclaimed the everlasting standard for entrance to the church: "Repent, and be baptized every one of you in the name of Jesus Christ for the remission of sins" (Acts 2:37-38). Gospel preaching was the key to the door of the church that day, and any day, and broken hearts and contrite spirits were, and are, the passport through that door. The other day I asked a little boy of six, "How do you get into the church?" and he replied, "Come through the door!" I was stunned at the accuracy of his answer. No doubt, he was thinking of the church building, but he, nevertheless, told me the correct answer. Some people seek admittance to the church by other means than by the door. Jesus said, "He that entereth not by the door into the sheepfold [church], but climbeth up some other way, the same is a thief and a robber. . . . I am the door: by me if any man enter in, he shall be saved" (John 10:1, 9). Christ is the only possible entrance to the Bible church.

I know what you mean, Morton, when you speak of a minister opening the door to the church. I recall being in a church that used the same method, but Christ said this is one that "climbeth up some other way." This idea that one may join the church by shaking the minister's hand and answering some questions, or by any other method than through an experience with God is not God's plan; it is only a substitute. God said through the Revelator, "Behold, I set before you an open door, and no man can shut it" (3:8). Furthermore, he said that Christ had the key, and he was the one who "openeth, and no man shutteth; and shutteth and no man openeth." The wide-open door to the church awaits everyone who humbly repents and accepts Christ as his Savior.

When people are added to an organization by man, though it be called a church, it is no longer God's church. A few years ago a committee of twenty-five top theologians of the world met in Geneva, Switzerland, to lay plans to meet the challenge of religion in the atomic age. They came up with this astounding pronouncement: "Our churches are sick." Of course, everyone already knew that the churches were sick, but these men studied the symptoms and pressed further with their diagnosis. Said they, "In many subtle ways the churches have capitulated to the temptation of worldliness." And they found the specific troubles of the church to be three in number.

First, the church now relies on the protection of the state. The early church had no such protection. Second, the church seeks the support of the wealthy. Third, the church depends on a particular form of civilization involving push buttons, gadgets, and all the accompaniments of ease. I mention these, Morton, for right here is what makes the church sick: men have joined all kinds of sinners to the Christian body, allowing them to occupy important positions in the church until it has become a man-made fellowship in place of the fellowship of the redeemed. The "many subtle ways" by which the church has capitulated to the temptation of worldliness include easy church joining. When men enter a church without sincerely seeking forgiveness from our Lord Jesus Christ, that church becomes a secular organization, though it may be called religious. To make up the true church men and women would necessarily have to be added as were the members of the early church. Then "the Lord added to the church daily such as should be saved" (Acts 2:47).

Some have substituted self-improvement for the new birth, but God is not one who merely improves the human heart. He is a God who *changes* the heart. He gives a new heart, a new mind, new motives, new desire, new purposes. Over and over I have heard people say, and so have you, Morton: "I am going to clean up. I am going to turn over a new leaf, be a good neighbor, a good citizen, live a respectable life, go to church, and live right." Yet never have I known one person to save himself by this self-improvement method. Before long he sinks back into the same old rut of sin.

Straightforward Jeremiah of the Old Testament days asked some pertinent questions relative to a self-made way of life: "Can the Ethiopian change his skin? Can a leopard change his spots?" Then he answered his own questions: "Then may ye also do good, that are accustomed to evil." Christ said, "Which of you . . . can add one cubit unto his stature?" Then he drives the nail, "Without me you can do nothing."

Still another says, "I will join a church, the best one I can find, and give my service, talents, and time there." That is a noble pledge, but the church today has "in many subtle ways . . . capitulated to the temptation of worldliness," being brought to that condition by so many of its leaders being just sinners dressed in a Sunday garb. Men still sing a two-thousand-year-old song. It goes like this: "We tithe, we fast, we pray, we go to church, we do good deeds, we help the poor." The Pharisees wrote both the words and the tune to that old song. Christ appraised it with these words: "Except your righteousness shall exceed the righteousness of the scribes and Pharisees, ye shall in no case enter into the kingdom of heaven" (Matt. 5:20).

Some seek a church group they like and just sit down and identify themselves with the group, never embracing or experiencing the spirit of the group. But to identify yourself with the church is not enough. As an illustration of this point, consider the elder brother of the Prodigal Son. He was at home with the family, but he was more lost and sinful than the Prodigal. The Prodigal suffered from sins of the flesh. The older brother was a member of the family, but all likeness to the father was purely incidental; he had nothing but identification. That is all some people have who sit in church every Sunday.

Remember the story Jesus told of the man who came to the wedding feast improperly dressed? "When the king came in to look at the guests, he saw there a man who had no wedding garment; and he said to him, 'Friend, how did you get in here without a wedding garment?' And he was speechless. Then the king said, . . . 'Bind him hand and foot, and cast him into the outer darkness; there men will weep and gnash their teeth' " (Matt. 22:11-13, RSV). You see, Morton, the eyes of the king sought out the man who had only identification, but had made no preparation for the occasion whatever. When the end comes and we are required to face the searching eyes of our Lord, we must have more than identification. Ananias and Sapphira identified themselves with the early church. They seemed like good people. They looked all right. But they were liars. You know the story. They were struck dead.

The first step toward becoming a member of the church

of God is for one to know that he is lost. "All have sinned, and come short of the glory of God" (Rom. 3:23). If you are a Christian, Morton, the minute you became a Christian, God added you to the church. But if you are not a Christian, it is necessary that you awake now to the fact that you are a sinner, that you are lost. If you were floating on a rubber raft on a stormy sea and did not realize the danger until the storm became so furious it was impossible to rescue you, it would then be too late to warn you of the danger. The transgressor, the sinner, is in a more precarious condition than a person on a rubber raft at sea. He is riding the high tide of sin, and sudden destruction is just ahead. Remember Paul:

> "Awake, O sleeper, and arise from the dead,
> and Christ will give you light" (Eph. 5:14, RSV)

However, it is not enough just to be aware that you are lost. You must be saved. And there is only one true way to be saved and added to the church. " 'The most significant contribution of the Church of God to world Christianity is its concept of church membership.' This opinion expressed by one of America's outstanding Christians, Dr. E. Stanley Jones, represents only one man's judgment, of course. But coming from a churchman of such stature and one not affiliated with the Church of God movement, it would seem to be an observation which would bear further investigation. Just what did Dr. Jones have in mind when he noted this concept of church membership, and what are its implications for world-wide Christianity?"*

Dr. Jones simply means that the Church of God movement has returned to the New Testament for instructions in

---

*From "Members of His Body," by John W. V. Smith, in the *Gospel Trumpet*.

becoming a member of the church. Again, I must say, Morton, if we should get our directions from any source other than the Bible we could not be right. It is evident that man must have the second birth. Jesus said no man can see the kingdom of God without the second birth, or, as he called it, being "born again" (John 3:3). We believe one becomes a member of the church of God when he experiences the new birth.

Morton, this illustration, though it is quite prosaic, may help you understand God's plan and show the fallacy of voting members into a church body. I am a member of a family of eight children; I happen to be the sixth child. Suppose on the day of my birth my father had gathered the other five children together and had exclaimed: "You have a new brother. Hillery was born today. Do you feel that we should vote him into our family?" Even those children would have said, "Why, Father, how could we vote him in? He is already here; he was born into our family!"

What if the family had voted on me? What if they had voted to reject me, and even destroyed my birth certificate? Would that have nullified my birth? I was still born! What if they had voted to accept me? Would that have made my birth any more valid? I was already born! Now, for one who is "born" into the family of God, would voting on him make him a better Christian? If a man is born again by the Spirit of God and is thus added to the church by the Lord, what bearing could the vote of human beings have upon it? Becoming a member of the church of God is a divine act between God and man, and the formulas of man have no effect upon that act.

When one learns that he is lost, he is ready to do business with Deity. He is too helpless a creature to save himself.

His bootstraps are too weak for him to lift himself by them out of his dilemma. His moral goodness and boasted righteousness are as filthy rags. But thank God, Morton, the sure cure is found, and here is man's part: "If we confess our sins, he is faithful and just to forgive us our sins, and to cleanse us from all unrighteousness" (I John 1:9). Who will forgive our sins? Christ Jesus, the Son of God. "The blood of Jesus Christ his Son cleanseth us from all sin" (vs. 7).

No man has to beg the Lord for the experience of the new birth; no one has to wait until God is in the right frame of mind. A knowledge of our lost state, a broken heart and a contrite spirit, and a willingness to surrender to God and his plan are the only terms we need to meet. "God . . . is a rewarder of them that diligently seek him" (Heb. 11:6). So, Morton, if one desires God's fellowship, his pardoning love, and the privilege of communing with Him more than he desires anything else, he is at the very door of the kingdom of heaven, ready to be added to the church. But no man will ever stumble accidentally into the church of God. Only those who seek God with all their hearts find him. "God is a rewarder of them that diligently seek him." Those of feeble effort cannot enter.

Anyone who comes to the state of confessing his sins has first been sensitive to the gospel. The gospel has convicted him of sin and has pointed him to the true door of the church. And at this hour of decision he is ready to repent. "Repent," Morton, means, literally, to turn around and go the other way. Therefore, this repentance must go deep— deep into the heart and conscience. The man who claims to repent and makes only a quarter turn, or a half turn, is in for trouble. In the process of repenting he must "turn around" completely and go a new way.

In some religious circles there is a decided hesitancy to dwell on the need of repentance; hence we have many who claim to have repented, and yet their lives have not been changed. A recent writer says, "Repentance is a radical orientation of life around a new center, and faith is spiritual receptivity." Imagine, if you can, John the Baptist telling his listeners to reorient their lives around a new center, or Paul telling the Philippian jailer to exercise "spiritual receptivity." The preaching of Bible truth draws men to repentance. God's love as revealed in Christ, his judgment on sin, his demands for righteous living—these truths turn men's hearts to repentance. The result of repentance to Paul meant that "if any man be in Christ, he is a new creature: old things are passed away; behold, all things are become new" (II Cor. 5:17). When a man repents, turns around, goes the other way, God can make him a new creature. "Behold, all things are become new!"

Morton, the door to the church is anything but wide to some people. This is true because they want to enter the church with a quarter-turn experience. They are not willing to repent wholeheartedly, and let their whole being be made new. Jesus said that a camel could more easily squeeze through the eye of a needle than could some people get into the church. It is laughable to consider a camel going through the eye of a needle, and it is ridiculous that some would seek admittance to the church halfheartedly, unwilling to throw off every weight and strip for the Christian race.

This little story, "The Camel," illustrates what I mean:

I loaded my camel rich and high, and marched him up to the needle's eye. He was laden with riches manifold, with bales of silk and sacks of gold, with precious stones and with jewels rare, and with vessels lovely be-

yond compare. I hoped to enter with all my gain, but the needle's eye made my efforts vain. I urged my camel with angry din; I pressed the camel to enter in. But far too large with his loading high, he could not pass the needle's eye.

I rode the camel a night and a day, and sought to enter some other way; but though I followed a wearisome round, only the needle way I found. I groaned, for I did not have enough; but I took from the camel my bulkier stuff, and with gold and gems I would fain get by. Still, the camel stuck at the needle's eye. Then I left the camel alone outside, and with only my gems again I tried. All of my pockets stuffed—alas—the needle still I could not pass.

Then at length I threw my wealth away and sank upon lowly knees to pray. I begged the Lord to forgive my sin and let a poor hapless traveler in. Then proud and glad, in beggar's dress, I passed the portal of happiness.

The simple truth, Morton, is that the doors of the church of God are closed to sin in any form. Confessing our sins, repenting, and accepting the saving grace of Christ must of necessity include the forsaking of sin. That means to throw away all pursuits that exclude God. "What things were gain to me, those I counted loss for Christ" (Phil. 3:7).

Therefore, Morton, God's design for salvation, for becoming a member of his church, is through the hearing of the gospel, conviction of our sins, repentance, and acceptance of pardon, or forgiveness. We become a member through the new birth—that is, by a change of heart, a change of life and living. It is a matter of being added to the church by the Lord and not by any man.

Some people have a difficult time believing and accepting, but God is eager to do great things for the obedient. Obedience breaks down wrong patterns of living. It takes wholehearted surrender, complete trust and obedience to enter the church. Christ said to the man with the withered hand, "Stretch forth thy hand." That was just what the poor man could not do, but I think there must have been something in the face and voice of Jesus that made the man think, "If he tells me to do it, I can." When the man made the effort to stretch forth his hand he found that he *could*. I have known those who said, "I would like to find God, become a member of the church, but my surroundings, my situations, my handicaps—I just can't." But when they tried they found they could. Obedience does the impossible.

To the broken, impotent man, Christ said, "Rise, take up thy bed, and walk." Nothing was more impossible for this man to do than this, but when he made the effort, by God's grace he found that he could. And he who came with his back on the bed went out with the bed on his back. A woman said to me some time ago, "I just cannot repent; I am bound by filthy habits and unclean living." But she made an effort and found that she could, and she did. She became a member of the church of God that very hour.

Then, when one has heard the Word, experienced its convicting power, confessed, repented, accepted God's pardon, and turned his back on sin, he is a member of the church of God. An American soldier was shot down on a Japanese battlefield in World War II with a slug in his neck. While lying in his own blood, dying, with the wind blowing and the rain pouring down upon him, six thousand miles from home and loved ones, he managed to get a piece of paper from his pocket, and a short pencil. He scribbled something, and then died. When his friends found him the piece of paper was clasped tightly in his hand. On it were these words: "Peace like a river." Morton, that is what every man wants, "peace like a river," and he may find that peace by accepting the Bible plan of salvation, which gives him membership in the church.

Morton, I shall be praying that as you read this letter God's Spirit will in a special way illumine your heart and mind and give you the understanding in this important matter of church membership that you seem to want so much.

Sincerely,

HILLERY

10

WHY USE THE NAME, CHURCH OF GOD?

DEAR MORTON:

I am not surprised at your answer to my last letter on how to become a member of the church of God. You wrote, "My experience harmonizes perfectly with your explanation. I was a member of the church of God and did not know it. . . . I am so happy that I do not have to go through some man-made ritual to be a member of God's church."

Furthermore, you state, "I notice there are so many church groups bearing so many different names. What is the right name for the Bible church? Should it always be the church of God? I have been told that it matters not what name a church may bear, for we are all heading for the same place. Where did all these names originate? Where did the title 'Church of God' originate? Why do we use it? Are the many names and titles of church groups biblical? Please set me straight on the right Bible name for the church."

Morton, the true church is made up, not of brick, stone, or wood, or any such things, but of people with pure hearts and minds. The church is not a political system which exercises authority over millions, but a simple fellowship of believers in Christ, existing to glorify God and to serve each other and the needy. It is not a mere organization being perpetuated for its own sake, but an organism dedicated to

102

the proclamation and spread of the gospel of Christ, which is the power of God unto salvation to all people. Surely, such an organization could not possibly be named by man.

First, let us examine some names of religious groups today, and then ascertain their origin. To show that the many names or titles used by the some 250 religious groups today are man-designed, it will be necessary that I mention names. It is not my intention to make derogatory remarks about any religious group, for almost all of them have made large contributions to Protestant religion. However, the fact that a religious organization has greatly enriched Christendom does not validate its man-made name.

About the most confused person of whom we have an account in the Bible is the Gadarene. He had left his family to live in a cemetery. He was so confused and wild that no one could tame him. He was a split personality, if ever there was one. Jesus "asked him, What is thy name? And he answered, saying, My name is Legion: for we are many" (Mark 5:9). I do not attribute all the church names to the enemy, but I do believe he uses them to divide the body of Christ.

Surely Christendom could say today, "My name is legion [six thousand]. There are many persons in me, pulling in opposite directions, many clamorous voices in the town meeting of the mind, with no gavel in the hands of a powerful chairman to bring them to order!" Our name is Legion, but the New Testament has a sure cure for that: "I . . . will give him a white stone, and in the stone a new name written" (Rev. 2:17). That name is clearly written, the church of God.

Our present-day religious bodies have secured their names in a variety of ways. The Lutheran groups get their name from their founder, Martin Luther. John Wesley's followers came to be known as Methodists because of their orderly or methodical way of studying and organizing. The Adventist groups get their name from a particular teaching on the second coming of Christ which they emphasize. The Quakers have made respectable a term originally applied to them in derision. However, none of these titles comes from the Bible, and rarely does a person using one of these names claim that it is the appropriate name for the whole church.

The New Testament calls the individual followers of Christ friends, disciples, brethren, saints, Christians. For example, "The disciples were called Christians first in Antioch" (Acts 11:26). But as a church the believers took the name of their Father, the church of God.

Morton, I am sure you can see now how the many titles and names for the many church groups originated. Often a religious group was named for some ambitious Christian leader. Sometimes the name came from a Bible term. At times the methods of a group gave birth to their name. However, if we go to the Bible for our plan of salvation and the doctrines of the church, why would it not be logical to go there for its name, also? While I do not believe that those who furnished the various names for religious groups had in mind to divide the body of Christ, the true church, yet I do believe the enemy of the church employs these many titles to divide the body of Christians around the world. I have seen those who manifest a deeper respect for the name of their group than they do for their Lord.

Morton, one cannot help noticing the change in Christendom since the Day of Pentecost, the dedication day of the church. On that memorable day men were saved by repentance of their sins and acceptance of Christ into their hearts.

Today there are multiple ways of becoming Christian, so they say. The first-century Christians believed and practiced a clean and pure life. Today, it is not unusual to hear one profess Christ one minute and curse in his name the next. The first church had a specific name, clearly marked in the Bible; today, we have churches of many, many names. It is evident that the masses are satisfied with a second-best experience of salvation, and they are content with a man-made name for the church.

How utterly unchristian for man to formulate his own commandments and call them Christian, organize his group after a secular plan, and stamp a man-made name on it and call it the body of Christ, the church. It would be strange, indeed, that Christ would build his church, give it a Bible name, and then be pleased that man has titled it with scores of names. Only a person who is filled with God's Spirit, who is on fire for God, and who enjoys a New Testament experience of holy living can ever discern the imperativeness of following the whole New Testament pattern for the church. This is true, also, in regard to the name of the church.

Isaiah, prophesying of the church hundreds of years before Christ, said, "Thou shalt be called by a new name which the mouth of the Lord shall name" (62:2). In his high priestly prayer, Christ prayed, "Holy Father, keep them in thy name which thou hast given me, that they may be one, even as we are one" (John 17:11, RSV). Christ desires that the church be one and be called by one name, "that the world may believe." More than one sincere person has said to me, "All the many names of church groups confuse me. How could anyone know which group is right?" Christendom is not on the earth to confuse, but rather to compel men to come to Christ. Of course, the many names given to church groups are not the major cause of schism in the body of Christ; nevertheless, they contribute to the confusion in the church.

Thousands and thousands of Bible students today read Christ's great prayer, recorded in John 17, and yet division and confusion continue. But the apostles believed Christ's prayer to be divine; they sought to make it come true. One of these apostles said, "Feed the church of God, which he hath purchased with his own blood" (Acts 20:28). These early churchmen knew no other name for the church. Morton, Paul, one of the greatest men of New Testament times, was a church of God preacher and wrote the church at Galatia to that effect. He said, "I persecuted the church of God violently and tried to destroy it." Then, after he was saved by the grace of Christ Jesus, he declared that he was "now preaching the faith he once tried to destroy." (Read Galatians 1 in Phillips' modern speech translation.)

A dozen times throughout the New Testament "church of God" is used to designate the Bible name for the Bible church. Morton, please check these references: I Corinthians 1:2; 10:32; 11:22; 15:9; Galatians 1:13; I Timothy 3:5; II Corinthians 1:1.

"Men moved by the Holy Spirit spoke from God" (II Pet. 1:21, RSV) concerning the organization of God's church. They told us how to become members of this church; they even wrote the message for the church of God. Does it seem possible that they would not tell us the true name of that church? If I were directed to a certain city in India, informed about its people, their customs, its location, and yet was not told the name of the city, would I not be in a state of confusion?

The word "church" has become a generic term. We have

the A—— church, the B—— church, and the C—— church, and each one has a distinct doctrine and name. And the peculiar doctrine and name of each organization make a separating wall between it and other religious groups. Hence, we have a terribly disturbed and divided Christendom. But as we leaf the pages of the Bible, we find only *one* church with *one* name. Just as the carpenter and the manufacturer have blueprints and patterns to guide them, so we must have a norm or measuring stick by which we determine what is the true church. All who believe in Christ must concede the Bible to be our guidebook, our blueprint.

As stated before, there are scores of organizations today, the members of each contending that they are *the* church. The writer of Revelation referred to the church as "the Bride, the wife of the Lamb" (21:9, RSV). Then, the right church is Christ's bride. It would be sinful even to infer that Christ would return for more than one bride, and to assert such would be blasphemy. Paul spoke of the church as being Christ's body (Eph. 1:22-23). It would be sheer foolishness to imagine that Christ is to return for two bodies. We must conclude that Christ will not return for ten churches, bearing ten different names, not even two, but for *one* church —his body, his bride.

It is a fact today that there are more than 250 religious organizations, each one claiming to preach the pure gospel of the Lord. If that be true, what right do I have, Morton, to select one from that number and designate it as *the* church? I have none, but I can search the Word of God, which is the highest authority in the Bible church. Was Paul overstepping his privilege when he wrote, "Unto the church of God, which is at Corinth" (I Cor. 1:2)? Of course, some will say, "All Christians are members of the church of

God." And that is true, but just in part. It is true relative to the *universal* phase of the church, but God's church is so designed that there is also a local phase. When Paul wrote, "Unto the church of God, which is at Corinth," he was addressing a specific people in a definite location, whose members, being redeemed by faith in Christ, met together for worship and were accepted by each other on the grounds of their experience with God.

Three hundred years before the Roman Catholic Church was established, and fifteen hundred years preceding the organization of the first Protestant church, Paul wrote, "Beyond measure I persecuted the church of God" (Gal. 1:13). In the same chapter we read, "He which persecuted us in time past now preacheth the faith which once he destroyed" (vss. 23-24). As I stated above, Paul was a church of God preacher; once he persecuted the church of God, later he preached it. To the Ephesians the same Paul wrote, "I bow my knees unto the Father of our Lord Jesus Christ, of whom the whole family in heaven and earth is named" (3:14-15). If all the saints in heaven and on earth bear the name of the Father of our Lord why should men give secular names to religious bodies and call them *the* church? Just to call a group the "Church of God" does not necessarily make it so; but, if it is the church of God, let's title it so.

Had I gone to the home of a Mr. Brown and asked that I might bear his name and become a member of the Brown family, my father would have felt that I despised his name. I have always felt that men who change their names certainly have little respect for them. When man joins some organization bearing some other name than that of God, surely God is displeased with him. But some will say, "There is nothing in a name." If that be true, why not bear a different name at the shop where we work, at the grocery store where we purchase our food, and at the church where we pay our tithes? That would be confusing, would it not? But there is something in a name. Says Goethe, "A man's name is not like a mantle which one perchance may safely twitch and pull, but a perfectly fitting garment, which, like the skin, has grown over him, at which one cannot rake and scrape without injuring the man himself." The same reverence and respect for the name of the true church must be employed. Change the name of the church, and much of its identity is lost. Christ left no phase of his church to chance or luck. Before his crucifixion he prayed that we might bear his Father's name, and when he returns and finds folks joined to organizations not so much as mentioned in his Word, he will not be pleased.

Paul heralded the name church of God everywhere he went. I am aware, Morton, that "church of Christ" is used once in the New Testament (Rom. 16:16), where Paul says, "The churches of Christ salute you." The apostle was not changing the name of the church; he was merely recognizing that all the congregations belonged to Christ.

Morton, there is one danger I must avoid. Let me make it clear that we do not believe that the movement we term the Church of God today contains all Christian people. We realize and proclaim that all born-again people are members of the great universal church of God, but does it not seem strange, Morton, that we should search the Scriptures for instructions in all matters pertaining to the church, and then go elsewhere for the name of that church? Just as the mode of entrance into the church, the government of the church, the instructions for righteous living in the church, and other important issues have been corrupted or changed, so has the name of the church.

The Bible instructs Christians, "Whatsoever ye do, do all to the glory of God; . . . glorify God in your body, and in your spirit, which are God's" (I Cor. 10:31; 6:20); "Let your light so shine before men that they may see your good works, and glorify your Father which is in heaven" (Matt. 5:16). Therefore, it is only good sense that the church should bear the title which honors and glorifies God and distinguishes it as belonging to him.

We must conclude, Morton, that Roman Catholics are absolutely wrong in setting up a nonbiblical system of doctrine, practice, and membership and insisting that it and it alone is the true church. Protestantism has not helped the situation by breaking the body of Christ into 250 segments, bearing many names. We must return to the New Testament for the right name of the church, which is church of God, just as we give all authority to the New Testament for instructions in all other matters of the plan of God. The Church of God movement happily proclaims and practices this truth.

Morton, I sincerely hope that this letter will help you to see how the many church groups received their names, where the name "church of God" originated, and why we use the term today. I shall be waiting to hear from you again soon.

Sincerely,
HILLERY